ROADSIDE FOOD

ROADSIDE FOOD

GOOD HOME-STYLE COOKING ACROSS AMERICA

Photographs by LeRoy Woodson, Jr.

Text by
Jill MacNeice
Schuyler Ingle
Ralph Gardner, Jr.
Russell Martin
LeRoy Woodson, Jr.
J.C. Suarès
Timothy White
John Sturman
Barbara Ottenhoff
Roy Finamore
Matthew Klein

Stewart, Tabori and Chang
New York

Front cover photograph by LeRoy Woodson, Jr.
Back cover photograph by Matthew Klein.
Frontispiece by Cindy Lewis. Copyright ©1986, 1982 Stewart, Tabori & Chang.
Chapter opening photographs by Matthew Klein. Copyright
©1986 Stewart, Tabori & Chang, Inc.
Chapter opening prop styling by Linda Cheverton; food styling by Andrea Swenson.
"Ham and Eggs" by Schuyler Ingle is adapted from an article
that appeared in *The Weekly*, Seattle, Washington.

Special thanks to Jeff Stoker.

Published by Stewart, Tabori & Chang, Inc.
740 Broadway, New York, New York 10003

Library of Congress Cataloging-in-Publication Data

Woodson, LeRoy.
    Roadside food.

    1. Gastronomy.   2. Diet—United States.   3. Restau-
rants, lunch rooms, etc.—United States.   4. Cookery,
American.   I. Finamore, Roy.   II. Title.
TX633.W66   1986   641'.01'3   85-30254
ISBN 0-941434-68-0 (pbk.)

Distributed by Workman Publishing
1 West 39th Street, New York, New York 10018

Printed in Spain

86 87 88 89 10 9 8 7 6 5 4 3 2 1

First Edition

❖❖❖❖❖❖❖❖❖❖❖ **TODAY'S SUGGESTIONS** ❖❖❖❖❖❖❖❖❖❖❖

❖❖❖❖❖❖❖❖❖ **INTRODUCTION** ❖❖❖❖❖❖❖❖❖❖

There is, undoubtedly, a classic American dining experience: discovering the ideal roadside restaurant. Here, the setting is simple, the waitress is friendly, the grillman is a wiseacre with the coordination of a blackjack dealer, and the food is good and it's cheap and there's lots of it. Even the clientele plays a role: the state trooper sitting at the counter and the truck drivers in a nearby booth give the place a ring of authenticity.

I remember finding just such a place. I was seventeen, a freshman in college, and the temporary owner of my father's convertible. Warm spring nights, after a quick cram for a chemistry exam, I would drive through the Virginia hills in search of Sweetbriar girls, and sometimes I found them. I also found the University Diner in Charlottesville. It was a classic diner, cast in the phoney "trolley car" mold, with a counter that ran the length of the restaurant and seven wobbly stools. The rest of the seating consisted of miserably uncomfortable wooden booths against the opposite wall. There were jukeboxes, of course—little ones in each of the booths—and at least five calendars on the wall.

I don't remember what the menu looked like, I'm not sure I ever even saw it. I do remember that night after night I ended up at the University Diner for "breakfast," and I always ordered the same thing: two eggs over easy (the deep-orange yolks never broken), hash (with recognizable chunks of beef), thick slices of toasted white bread (served with a soupbowl of orange marmalade), and a bottomless cup of strong black coffee. All of this was dished up by a waitress who seemed to care about my meal, and it cost less than a dollar.

By the time I graduated, change had crept in. The University Diner was now many times its original size, a modern wonder of polished aluminum and sleek glass, with a staff the size of a football team. The food had changed too—it had lost that special home-cooked taste and appearance. There had been a time when I could sit at the counter and the waitress would call out my order without my having said a word. No longer.

The head and handle of William the Conqueror's battle axe have changed many, many times, but it's still William the Conqueror's battle axe. And in my memory, the University Diner is still the University Diner, its former identity intact. Such a microcosm of basic American honesty, ingenuity, generosity, and good cheer must never be lost.

It is the pursuit of such ideals that inspired this book. Photographer Le-Roy Woodson traveled 20,000 miles by car across America shooting and eating in restaurants, cafés, diners, and roadhouses that he discovered by chance and by recommendations from local people and those who make their living moving up and down the highways. Woodson and the ten other writers share this love of the diner with me, and they have written about their own experiences of finding and enjoying roadside food. We hope that every reader of this book has had the kind of eating experience that we so enjoy or, if not, that this book will lead to its fulfillment.

Andrew Stewart

DOUGHNUTS

by Jill MacNeice

When you've been driving since dawn, playing leapfrog with the big rigs while the radio's blaring country music, and your throat's craving a hot cup of coffee and something sweet to go with, and your car crests the rolling hills of Rockingham County, Virginia, you know you're in the right place for a doughnut break. The cows are a dead giveaway: Where there are cows there are farms, and farm folk are particular when it comes to doughnuts and pies and other such things as go with coffee or a cold glass of milk. This is a Mennonite area (complete with horse-drawn buggies), and the competition in baked goods is fierce; when a boy, especially a Mennonite boy, is moved to compare a restaurant doughnut or pie to his momma's, he's saying something. More likely than not, his momma's baking is so good she wouldn't even think of selling it, let alone entering it in a contest at the State Fair, because the best things in life are the ones you give away free.

As it turns out, some of the Mennonite boys in the community have made just such a comparison after eating at the Thomas House Restaurant and Air Conditioned Home Bakery across from the Marval turkey packing plant on Route 24 in Dayton. Lottie Thomas, who's been running the place for forty-two years and who was born and raised on a farm, takes it all in stride. "The farm hands that come in here, they don't make a big to-do because they all have good cooks at home," she says.

14

The gentle farm country of Rockingham County, Virginia, is the home of the Thomas House Restaurant and Home Bakery.

As soon as you step inside the Thomas House Restaurant and Air Conditioned Home Bakery, where ladies in flowered dresses and aprons serve up things like country fried ham with lima beans and sweet potatoes and home-made bread cafeteria-style for $4 and where you sit on gray metal folding chairs in a room that has got to have the biggest collection of memorial plates in Rockingham County, you figure you're in for some mythical, no-nonsense roadside food, because there aren't any fine table linens, or waiters who tell you their first name without asking yours, or fresh cut flowers in French mineral water bottles to distract. As Mrs. Thomas says, she'd have to charge too much to pay for them, and "anyways, the kind of people that comes here don't care nothing about all that fancy extrey stuff like tablecloths and nice chairs."

Not that Mrs. Thomas is cheap. It's just that she knows what's important, and things like good food and air conditioning are at the top of the list. Even if it didn't say so on the sign (which draws drivers from the road like deer to a salt lick), there's no denying that the place is air conditioned—as a matter of fact, it's downright cool inside. Mrs. Thomas will tell you right off that she was the first person in the Valley to put in air conditioning and that was over forty years ago, when the place was still just a bakery. Of course, you can't eat air conditioning, but you can eat her doughnuts and desserts, and you'd be a fool not to.

They've got glazed doughnuts, which they used to fry up fresh every day but which now, as a rule, they make only on Mondays, Wednesdays, and Fridays. And then there are cream-filled varieties and chocolate doughnuts and, every once in a while, cake doughnuts with banana filling. If you want a doughnut on a Tuesday, Thursday, or a weekend, Mrs. Thomas will put a frozen one in the microwave for you, to melt the glaze to the proper stickiness. Then again, you may not even want a doughnut once you get a look at the pies: There's fresh apple pie and blueberry pie and peach pie and rhubarb pie, which is flavored with concentrated orange juice because it tastes better that way, and lemon pie, cream pie, coconut pie, custard pie made with fresh milk and eggs, chocolate pie, butterscotch pie, and even peanut butter pie, which Mrs. Thomas found in a cookbook, although the other recipes are original. Then you have cobblers, which you eat smothered in what they call Country Cream ("Ethel, we got any more of that fresh Country Cream?"), and banana pudding, which is never pronounced with the "g," and a carrot cake the likes of which they wouldn't allow in New York City because standing in line for it would likely start riots, and apple cake, and fresh fruit salad or a bowl of sugared blueberries with whipped cream, and a dish known as fried apples, which they claim is a vegetable but would pass for dessert without trying too hard, especially with some of that fresh Country Cream to go on top.

Having sampled both the doughnuts and the pies, I'd be hard-pressed to choose between them, although I'd say if you pull in during the A.M., particularly a Monday, Wednesday, or Friday A.M., you might as well head for the fresh fried doughnuts, which will run you a quarter each, and if you arrive in the P.M. you should go for the pie, which costs $.75 a slice for plain fruit ones and $.85 for the more elaborate models.

If you have spent any time eating doughnuts in roadside restaurants, I don't have to tell you that the world is divided into two kinds of people: those who dunk their doughnuts in their coffee and those who don't. I belong to the latter group and so do most of my friends, although my cousin Mary Mae used to dunk her peanut butter and jelly sandwich in her chocolate milk, and I dipped Oreos in milk before I knew better. According to my friend Wayland, a transplanted country boy who hails from Wise, Virginia, and who once spent some time in Rockingham County when his car broke down, you can't trust a man

The Thomas House has been serving no-nonsense, home-style roadside food for nearly fifty years.

who dunks because anybody who would do a thing like that out in public would steal money from the Salvation Army on Christmas Eve without batting an eyelash. I consider Wayland an expert in doughnuts because he takes them seriously; he has sworn oaths on them when the occasion warrants. ("Take a flying leap through a rolling doughnut.") Wayland wouldn't think of starting a day on the road without a doughnut and a cup of coffee.

My friend Mark, who also claims to be a doughnut expert but who really specializes in blueberry pancakes, maintains that dunking is a way to ruin both a good cup of coffee and a good doughnut, although he will often try a quick dip just to see if the doughnuts have staying power, that being the ability to hold hot coffee without going all to bits. There is nothing worse—and your dunkers will agree with this—than a layer of undifferentiated doughnut muck at the bottom of your coffee cup.

To give dunkers their due, the act comes from a long, and what I consider honorable, tradition of mopping up gravies and sauces with bread. And it takes a certain culinary adventurousness to combine the sweet with the bitter, the dry with the wet. But I don't buy the argument that it's okay to dunk because it gets all mixed up in the stomach anyway. That's like saying you should put chocolate icing on fried chicken.

It was Michael, an otherwise perfectly respectable man who sells TV sets for a living, who straightened me out on the subject. Michael makes it a point to stop in every roadside joint he thinks will deliver a decent doughnut. As Michael sees it, a roadside restaurant that is likely to have good doughnuts is just as likely to have bad coffee, so dunking is a way of making the coffee interesting. He has a point: The coffee at the Thomas House Restaurant and Air Conditioned Home Bakery is no great shakes. (The corollary to this is that when you're eating a stale doughnut you may as well dunk it to complete the transgression.)

The food historian William Woys Weaver says dunking was all the rage in Europe until the late 1800s and that the Pennsylvania Ger-

Preceding overleaf: Commemorative plates, depicting such events as the sinking of the battleship *Arizona* at Pearl Harbor, cover one wall of the Thomas House dining room.

Maria Maurogiorgos does most of the baking at the Thomas House—from bread and dinner rolls to doughnuts and pies.

mans still dunk just about everything that fits in a coffee cup and even eat something for breakfast called "Kaffe-Brocke"—a sort of coffee soup with bits of broken doughnuts floating in it. Mr. Weaver told me some interesting facts about the history of doughnuts, and I'd like to take a moment to clear matters up once and for all.

First, doughnuts were not invented in Camden, Maine, in 1847 by Hansen Gregory, as is popularly believed. Depending on which account you hear, Gregory was a sea captain, *or* a fifteen-year-old baker's apprentice who cut holes in doughnuts because he couldn't stomach the uncooked centers. Right away the discrepancies should tell you you're not getting the truth. Mr. Weaver says fried cakes, with and without holes, have been around for a very long time; the Romans even ate a kind of doughnut with the middle cut out (although they probably didn't roll them in powdered sugar and definitely didn't dunk them because coffee wasn't even invented yet). We know this because a fellow named Isidore of Seville, who lived in the fourth century A.D., mentioned fried dough in his writings.

In the Middle Ages doughnuts were an upper-class treat because they were expensive and complicated to make over an open hearth, but their popularity spread with the rise of the middle classes, and by the nineteenth century doughnuts were as commonplace as they are today. A lady named Hannah Glasse, the Betty Crocker of Edwardian England, had a recipe for doughnuts, which she called "Fried Jumbles," in her best-selling cookbook.

Secondly, there are no "nuts" in "doughnuts." Fried dough has appeared in different forms—round, square, triangular, twisted—under many different names. The Dutch settlers had *olykoeks* (oily cakes); the French in Louisiana had *beignets*; the Spanish from Mexico made *puchas de canela*; and the Pennsylvania Germans made *fastnachts* around Lent. The word doughnut comes from "dough knot," which was used in seventeenth-century England because the dough was knotted. It was shortened to "doughnut" because people got lazy, the way they're getting lazy about writing the word "doughnut" full out and are shortening it to "donut."

Dough is measured out by hand, eye, and an ancient scale, as Maria Maurogiorgos prepares fresh bread (left). To make the doughnuts, she rolls out a portion of dough and cuts it with a special doughnut cutter. Then, using a long wooden stick, she drops the rings into a deep fryer, turning them once. She scoops them up with the stick and hangs them to dry on a rack. Finally, she pours glaze over the doughnuts as they cool.

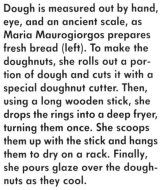

History notwithstanding, I'm inclined to keep the coffee and the doughnut separate, except in a limited number of instances, those being: 1) if you've never done it before and you want to prove to yourself that there's no need to dunk; 2) if the coffee's awful (see above); 3) if you're eating one of those cake doughnuts that nobody in their right mind would eat anyway because they are so dry and crumbly you couldn't possibly get it down unless it was soaked in coffee; 4) if you're Pennsylvania German (see above) or French. I've seen the French dunk their croissants in coffee and not even care that the melted butter has congealed at the top of the cup like scum on a pond.

Experts in the field argue widely about what makes a good doughnut. Wayland, who ate two glazed doughnuts for breakfast every working day between 1968 and 1982 from Blackie's Crystal Restaurant in Crystal City, Virginia, where he says they made the world's best doughnuts until they went belly up and it wasn't because their doughnut trade was slack, maintains the best doughnut will attempt to re-form itself in your stomach after you've eaten. (Some people, myself included, might call that indigestion.) Wayland also likes his doughnuts kind of slick on the inside. Those are his words exactly. Wayland feels strongly, and he'll argue it late into the night, that a doughnut is little more than a vehicle for glaze, which should be plenty sweet and transparent as suntan oil on a bathing beauty.

Mark, on the other hand, says the glaze should be ancillary to the doughnut proper, which should have an identifiable presence and taste, unless the doughnut is bad to begin with, in which case, all you have is the glaze, so it might as well be overpowering. He insists that doughnuts should be still warm when eaten to get the proper effect. Michael, who eats powdered, not glazed, doughnuts so he can dunk them (you can't dunk a glazed doughnut because the coating comes loose and floats around like shingles in your coffee), likes them fried crunchy on the outside and as airy and light as possible on the inside. But then, he's a dunker, so you have to take what he says with a grain of salt. As for myself, I'm partial to doughnuts that are not too heavy and not too sweet, and it it's "slicky" inside I'd rather give it to Wayland than eat it myself, since he appreciates that sort of thing.

What all these conflicting ideas about the constitution of a good doughnut have in common is the belief that doughnuts, whatever they are like, should have absolutely nothing to do with nutrition. They should, of course, be made with the finest natural ingredients, but the wholesomeness should stop then and there. Like demolition derbies, doughnuts are supposed to entertain. If you're looking to improve yourself while eating something sweet, buy a bran muffin, which is exactly what a lot of people are doing these days and why Dunkin' Donuts, the largest fried dough franchise in the country, has added a line of muffins and cookies to its offerings.

My friend Daniel, who lives in New York City and watches what he eats because he was heavy as a child, is a case in point. He is one of those people who love doughnuts but feel guilty about eating them, and yet wouldn't be caught dead eating a bran muffin. Fortunately, his psychiatrist is located right next to his favorite doughnut shop on Broadway between 86th and 87th, so he can go in and work off his bad feelings after indulging. Daniel is a true New Yorker and does not mince words. "Trash the Doughnut Hole!" he says. He's fully in favor of holes in doughnuts, but is opposed to eating Doughnut Holes, those little round things that are too small to sink your teeth into and have what he calls "too high a ratio of outside junk to inside junk."

The doughnut industry is understandably sensitive to this problem and not a little defensive about the image of the doughnut as a junk food hardly worth its 152 calories. "Make no mistake . . . the value of sweet goods and doughnuts is held in low esteem by consumers," says a recent article in a glossy industry magazine called *Bakery Production and Marketing*. The article attributes this deplorable state of affairs to the public's lack of knowledge about nutrition and urges bakers to "help them understand the dietary importance of baked goods." It's a bad sign indeed when even the doughnut makers are getting confused about their mission.

Between what's going on in the industry and people like my friend

A tranquil Sunday morning in Rockingham County, Virginia.

Opposite: Georgie Taylor, Juanita Michael, and Maria Maurogiorgos offer home-cooked food with a personal touch.

Daniel, I'm beginning to think William Woys Weaver is right when he says that the extinction of the doughnut as we know it could come sooner rather than later. He's seen it happen before: A food starts out among the upper classes and then becomes so ordinary after a few centuries that it falls out of fashion and soon everyone professes to hate it for one reason or another, sort of like rice pudding, which the nobility used to serve at weddings, but which you now mostly get in orphanages and old age homes. Or people try to doctor it up so that it seems more glamorous than it really is, like the shop in Los Angeles that sells chocolate glazed doughnuts sprinkled with chocolate chips and filled with peanut butter. You expect that sort of thing in California, where the Pacific Ocean stopped geographic expansion and caused the concept of frontier to take a sharp turn upward, into things like transcendent doughnuts and higher states of consciousness. But it's still appalling.

In the face of these and other undeniable signs of the Decline of the Doughnut in Western Civilization, places like the Thomas House Restaurant and Air Conditioned Home Bakery are the only hope for the continued existence of doughnuts fried honestly and without pretensions, whatever the fad in food. Which makes Lottie Thomas something of a curator in a living museum of food history.

Lottie Thomas' insistence on both ingredient and process tie her to the honorable tradition of doughnut making. She says it's important to have your ingredients (fresh eggs, flour, yeast, salt, shortening, sugar, and, for seasoning, mace and nutmeg), proportioned correctly. And, she says, "you can't have undermixin and you can't have overmixin, because if the dough's too tough, the doughnut's not fluffy; if it's too thin, it'll fail." And then you've got to have experience. She doesn't care what it is, yeast doughnuts or cake doughnuts, it takes experience to make a good one.

If you happen to be driving through Rockingham County, Virginia, near where Route 42 goes by the Marval turkey packing plant in Dayton, you can stop in at the Thomas House Restaurant and Air Conditioned Bakery and see for yourself.

HAM AND EGGS

by Schuyler Ingle

America owns breakfast, much as it owns jazz. Whether served with silver place settings in a fine hotel dining room or presented on paper place mats like the Tar Heel logger breakfasts dished out in timber-country diners in Washington State, it is the one restaurant meal this country has been able to define for the culinary world. It is the meal I like best, if only for its being so peculiarly private and personal in a public way. It is the meal that carries most of my childhood baggage as well as being the meal closest to dream time. Because of that I am appalled at the idea of power breakfasting, though in some business circles this is becoming quite the thing. What an awful way to start the day.

The British, I am certain, would agree. The British hold the most serious sub-lease on the restaurant breakfast as we know it, with an arsenal that includes beans on toast, gammon rashers, those dreadful bangers, poached eggs, kippers, scones, crumpets, marmalade, and oatmeal. Their Spam and eggs can match anything a Philadelphian can conjure up with Habersett scrapple. All the same, I can't imagine a British villain requesting Hangtown Fries before making his peace with the well-noosed rope.

I am suspicious of the French breakfast. It is best approached with the appetite of an old woman and a taste for desserts served first thing in the morning. Local hotels, inns, and bed and breakfast establishments that offer Continental Breakfasts always smell to me like they

A slice of Americana.

are getting away with something. Reduced to its most common components, the French breakfast is a thing of carbohydrates and stimulants. While it can be tasty, fun, romantic, even a diversion, it is an anemic afterthought when lined up against the honor roll of American breakfast options.

What stateside breakfast could be complete without, say, thick-cut bacon smoked long and lean with apple wood, then fried up out of the fat; hashbrowns cooked crisp on the outside so they are steamy and soft within; a couple of eggs slipped hot out of the pan right when the white part tightens up solid and leaves the yolk syrupy thick? The butter should roll over the top of the yolk and pool on the plate. The coffee in this exercise of definitives must be black, strong, hot, and come by the mug. The toast: make it from fresh-baked egg bread, please, ma'am. Or a good fresh white bread turned brown in the toaster then made limp with butter; jams and preserves served on the side. A monkey dish of stewed prunes. Fresh fruit if you have it: grapefruit or melon or berries when they are in season. Maybe a small steak leaking its juices into the bread-wiped smears of egg yolk. Count on biscuits in the South, creamed hominy, and ham. And sausage: round patties fried crisp with a message inside that reads sage, pepper, salt, and pork fat. You won't find pan-fried trout on your breakfast plate in an Italian dining room. And muesli is best left to the Swiss.

The problem here in Seattle—where to find good breakfast—is shared by cities across the country. Convenience has too often replaced good taste in centers of urban bustle. There is a generic breakfast out there on the loose, a thing shipped from a central warehouse on superhighways. An argument can be made that plastic food is the direct result of President Eisenhower's interstate highway construction program. Today it doesn't much matter if the restaurant in question is a greasy spoon, a chain monster made of molded foam, or a place of certain style, too often the breakfast is just more of the same. A suspicious man might think this soulless meal, a mere facsimile of relevant memory, has bird-dogged him from one side of the country to

Hattie's Hat in Seattle features Swedish pancakes with lingon-berries (Kim Zumwalt)

Overleaf: The only thing missing: two eggs any style.

the other, then all over town. But it is not a problem without a solution.

Simply look for the county two-lane, in spirit if not in kind. That's where you will find breakfasts that are alive and well and worth the wait. Seek out the diner that still serves breakfast all day and reestablish an intimacy with the basic American meal, the real thing. You won't regret taking the time to wander into Eugene, Oregon, to find the Old Pancake House rather than staying out there on the Interstate. True, you will lose a little time.

The Old Pancake House in Eugene is a twenty-one-year-old franchise of a Portland restaurant of the same name that has been around since the early 50s. Entire families have grown old together waiting in line for a shot at Dutch babies and apple pancakes, the house specialties. It takes 20 minutes to cook a Dutch baby, the custard-like egg batter started in an eight-inch frying pan on the grill, then flipped and popped into the oven to finish. It rises up like its own little mushroom cloud, and the waitresses jet from the kitchen past the Formica counters to whisk the sweet wonder out of the pan and onto a plate before it falls. With the taste of a Dutch baby lingering on your lips

Some patrons at Hattie's Hat are winding up for the day, and others are winding down. (Kim Zumwalt)

like the memory of a lover's kiss, a little time lost won't seem too significant. Even a bad breakfast that's real is better than one that's not.

My friend Siri Bardarson and I talked about all of this recently as we sat in Hattie's Hat in Ballard, waiting for our breakfast orders to appear. Ballard is the Scandinavian blue-collar neighborhood in Seattle, and in the area where Hattie's Hat is located the streets are paved with red brick. The last of the grand old hardware stores is just a couple of doors away, and down on the ship canal big crabbing boats and smaller fishing vessels have tied up for the winter. "After working all summer in salmon canneries up in Alaska," Siri said, "this is the place you want to come for breakfast. It helps you sort of ease back into the Lower 48."

I had asked for two eggs sunny side up with hashbrowns, white toast, and a salted black cod fillet on the side. (Have you *tried* to order white toast anywhere recently? Good luck.) Siri ordered Swedish pancakes with lingonberries. The waitress served a man at the table behind us an eight-ounce water glass filled with fizzing Alka-Seltzer. The boys at the bar (it's a magnificent sight to behold, a creation in ornately carved wood from another century and shipped around the Horn) were tipping back shooters of whiskey and schooners of beer to settle the shakes at the beginning of the day. In Hattie's Hat the current state of ham and eggs in America tends to take a back seat.

"Did your mom let you have all the bacon you wanted?" Siri asked in the middle of everything, and I couldn't tell her. It was an important question at seven in the morning, at breakfast, and I couldn't remember. But it seemed likely that my mother did. "I'd go over to my friend Marsha's house," Siri told me, "and her mom would cook all the bacon they could eat. A whole pound sometimes. My mom would cook eight slices. One slice for each of us five kids, one for her, and two for my dad. Can you beat that?"

James Beard loved bacon. At the Stanford Court in San Francisco

In Seattle, salted black cod is a popular side order at breakfast. (Kim Zumwalt)

he would order an entire plate of moderately broiled half-inch-thick bacon and call it breakfast. He developed a glaze that works best with the thick bacon sold in German delicatessens. You moisten a quarter cup of brown sugar to the consistency of a smooth paste with maybe a quarter cup of white wine, and then you add a teaspoon or two of Dijon mustard according to the dictates of your tastebuds. You lay out the bacon on foil on a baking sheet and slide it into an oven to bake until done, but not crisp. You could eat it then and there, but it would be pretty limp stuff. So you drain away the fat, and you brush the bacon with the glaze, and bake five minutes. Then you turn the bacon, brush the other side, and bake until crisp.

Ham is a whole other story. If you are lucky you will find a roadside cook cutting slices off a dry-cured, apple-wood-smoked expression of beauty and grace, like the hams from Methow Valley Meats in north central Washington State. Or one of those peppered hams from the Oregon coast. There is a cottage ham sold in southern British Columbia that is as close to the godhead as I may ever get. It is slightly salty and you aren't too likely to find it in any diners save the one closest to the smokehouse. Restaurant ham, for the most part, has been pumped full of water and no matter how it is cut and cooked, it will never come out right.

Good ham should be cut on the angle to achieve a thick slice with a thin edge. You don't want the pieces to be much more than three inches across. The good roadside cook will melt butter in a big, black iron skillet at moderate heat, then drop in the slices of ham while not allowing them to touch each other in the pan. If they do, they will steam and glaze. They won't be crisp, and that's what you want with your eggs, that variation in texture. Crank the heat up under the ham until the thin edge gets all brittle and brown. The salt concentrates here as well. When the ham is removed to a warm plate for serving, a little coffee is poured into the pan for red-eye gravy, a simple matter of de-glazing and reducing. That gives it all the chuckwagon bottom that true ham and eggs deserve, those juices of American reality.

I didn't eat eggs until I was sixteen. I'm still not partial to om-

No side orders are necessary with a spicy sausage omelet.

elettes. And when the wind is blowing just right, the smell of a soft-boiled egg scooped out of its shell can put me off my meal. I've settled on sunny side up as the way to go, and I know my luck's jake for the day when the eggs have been basted with butter.

Breakfast, of course, isn't always a thing of meat and eggs. Sometimes corn flakes will do just fine. You can order them for breakfast in India and except for the hot milk they serve with the cereal, you can almost close your eyes and taste your way back home. Siri was astonished when I told her as a kid I put the sugar on my cereal first, and that I floated my shredded wheat or corn flakes or wheat chex with half-and-half, not milk. "You were spoiled," she said. She agreed that the best part about family camping was eating cereal out of their little boxes split open down the middle. At home Siri had been inclined to spread butter on her shredded wheat, then sprinkle it with sugar and cinnamon, finally pouring on hot milk. That shredded wheat biscuit must have turned to mush in a minute.

Mush is what my grandfather used to call his breakfast cereal, whether hot oatmeal or crisp Cheerios. "Sit down and eat your mush," he'd say. He had been kicked in the face by a mule when he was young, and the only doctor around had been a barnyard vet, who was drunk and sewed him up with a needle and thread meant to suture a horse. So my grandfather's mouth sagged on one side where the scar tissue was heavy, and when he talked with a mouth full of shredded wheat, he'd sort of blow the stuff across the table, just a little.

I liked the eggs at Hattie's Hat, trading back and forth with bites of poached black cod fillet salty enough to startle the tastebuds. Siri thought the Swedish pancakes at Hattie's Hat were passably good, which is saying a lot. She grew up with a Swedish grandmother who made the real thing, turning them one at a time at the stove for her five grandchildren. "I'd look up at her," Siri says, "and think, 'This woman really loves me.'" A good restaurant breakfast has to incorporate some of that into the meal, or it's just another plate of ham and eggs.

My mother was always one to patiently slice sections of grapefruit completely free from the surrounding membrane. She'd do that for three children and my dad, having been the first one up. She'd flip the switch on the central heating on her way to the kitchen. She would cut the peels off oranges, slice the fruit into thin rounds, lay them out on a large plate, then sprinkle them with powdered sugar.

Her crowning glory, however, was blueberry pancakes when the bushes in the front yard were full of the fruit. She would leave the house dressed in a Stewart tartan wool bathrobe with a bowl in one hand and a long-shanked screwdriver in the other. On her way across the lawn she'd skewer long, fat slugs, stacking them up the length of the screwdriver. On her way back to the house with a bowl of blueberries, she'd stop at the garbage can, tip up the lid just enough to catch the edge of the screwdriver shaft, and with one quick pull, make a deposit.

What it all comes down to is a cook's big heart beating in the chest of whoever tends the grill. When the heart is there, you know it because the evidence is on the plate—and then it doesn't matter how long the drive. Don't just wolf down the real thing, then hit the road. And once ordered, breakfast is a meal to eat slowly, with concentration, with steady pacing.

My friend C. R. Roberts points out that he doesn't much remember lunches or dinners. "I'd be hard-put," he writes in a recent letter to me on the subject of breakfast, "to draw even a speculation as to what the main dinner course was, in Chicago, in Tacoma, even two weeks ago in Spokane. But I could describe how the table was set on the *Empire Builder*, how the silver shined, how the coffee steam rose at a breakfast I ate for four hours one morning, the train paralleling the Mississippi, random lines of *Huckleberry Finn* appearing in whispers; the breakfast in the old hotel in Helena when the waitress asked, 'You want hotcakes or toast?'" And that's it, really. Breakfast is there for taking time. Those ham and eggs don't just stick to your ribs, they stick to the rest of your life.

BURGERS

DRINK Coca-Cola

The Biltmore, the Plaza, the Royal and Ritz
May all have their popular joints and flitz
But after the show, when our money is low
We'll stick to the hamburger joints!

Greetings from Callaghan's Hotel, Wharton N. J.

by Ralph Gardner, Jr.

Some patriots get down on their knees and kiss the ground when they return to the United States. I go to my nearest Burger Heaven and order a cheeseburger deluxe. I employ the name "Burger Heaven" generically because the miracle of these little patties is that whether you happen to find yourself in one of the teeming center cities of the Northeast or a fishing village along the Oregon coast, chances are you're no more than fifty feet from a diner that makes a burger that'll put a smile on your face. Democratically priced, fast-cooking, and so flavorful it makes a mockery of the culinary pretenses of *haute* this and *nouvelle* that, the cheeseburger sings the praises of our republic more melodiously than any anthem.

As I take my place at the counter among my countrymen, the grillman—who serves as maitre d', chef de la cuisine, and confidant to his most faithful customers—places a paper napkin, knife, and fork in front of me. "What'll it be?" he growls. No time-consuming small talk here. This is not France but America, and language isn't an ornament but a tool. "A cheeseburger deluxe and a Coke," I grunt. It feels good to be back home.

In what other nation on earth could you order something as simple as a patty of ground beef "deluxe"? In Italy deluxe means dining on carpaccio and chianti in the antique twilight of Tuscany. In France it's a three-star restaurant and a thousand-franc bottle of wine. In Great Britain it's nothing less than being invited to sup with the

Opposite: There's no substitute for experience or the pride of ownership that distinguishes roadside restaurants.

Overleaf: Classic diner appointments make roadside dining a timeless experience at the White Manna in Hackensack, New Jersey.

Right and opposite: The White
Manna is an architectural jewel
that was built for the 1939
World's Fair as an example of
the diner genre.

Queen. Only in America is deluxe defined as a thimble-size cup of
cole slaw, a lettuce leaf with three slices of tomato, and a side of fries.
It's a manifestation of the American Dream, the belief that luxury is
accessible even to a man on a tight budget.

The grillman tosses the burger onto the grill and returns to his chores.
But don't let his nonchalance annoy you. If he's any good—and it's as
important that one find a first-class grillman as a good doctor or den-
tist—a timepiece as precise as the one at the Naval Observatory has
started ticking inside his head. (Two minutes a side for rare, three for
medium.) One stoolside companion recently noted that, "If they ask
you how you want it done, you know it's a bad sign." A good diner
chef simply knows instinctively when a burger is done. Besides, if
you wanted special treatment you should have gone to one of those
restaurants featured in *Architectural Digest* that charges $10 for
chilled cucumber soup.

   The burger hits the grill with a hiss. As fat and juice seep from its
pores, the noise builds toward a crescendo. My hunger makes me momentarily despondent. If somebody asked me to pass the ketchup at

this instant, I'd throw a punch.

The wisest thing to do is try to distract myself. It's probably the perfect time to raise a couple of controversial issues. The first is to wonder where Wendy's, McDonald's, and Burger King fit into the cheeseburger cosmos. Answer: They don't. It is impossible to separate a burger from its surroundings.

Part of the joy of dining out on burgers is that sense of belonging the customer feels, being part of the tumult at the counter. Like opera buffs on opening night, counter customers are ready to be dazzled by acts as simple as pouring a cup of coffee or cutting a tuna salad sandwich into two equal halves. A grillman with even the most rudimentary appreciation of show biz cannot help feeling some of the exhilaration of the soloist as he goes about his chores.

The performance of the chef at the local diner is in stark contrast to what goes on at those multinational burger machines where the act of creation is invisible; there's something sinister and totalitarian about a bushel of styrofoam-encapsulated Big Macs sitting under a heat lamp . . . orders filled even before they are placed. In the act of the grillman molding a burger to plump perfection, we see the modern world's equivalent of the medieval artisan. As he slaps and shapes the chopped meat, our host is transferring not only body heat to the burger but also a little love.

Take a look behind the counter and you will inevitably see the artifacts of a life dedicated to fast food—that first grease-stained dollar, picture calendars of Piraeus or some other port of origin of the grillman or his ancestors, and newspaper cartoons—yellow with heat and age—that sum up the daily ironies of a short-order cook's existence.

No matter how spotless the Formica and inoffensive the food at the chains, there is simply no way a photograph of a teenager with problem complexion over a plaque which reads "Employee of the Month" is going to convince me that that kid's personality is as wrapped up in the burger on the grill as that of a counterman who's devoted his life to his art.

Another issue I want to address is the nutritional value of burgers. In this age of amaretto tofutti and designer olive oils, the humble burger has come to be regarded by certain segments of the coat-and-tie crowd as somehow impure and, God forbid, passé. Rachel Carson I'm not, but I am well acquainted with the ecosystem that is my body, and when it comes to feeding myself, I subscribe to a single commandment—any food I craved as a kid is probably still very good for me. Years before my friends became music video directors, corporation PR men, or assistant professors acquiring tastes for osso bucco, sashimi, and other culinary affectations that any self-respecting little kid would cough into a napkin, they sat at my birthday parties in short pants, dribbling ketchup on themselves and joyously devouring cheeseburgers. It was as if, still tender from the womb, they could hear Mother Nature in all her inscrutable wisdom whisper, "Cheeseburgers are good for you. Cheeseburgers make you happy."

My burger is now jettisoning baby cannonballs of grease in all directions—evidence that it's ready for its encounter with that school-bus-yellow slab of American cheese. Fear grips me as I realize that the grillman, between making change and preparing a chocolate malted, has forgotten my burger. I become convinced that if he waits an instant longer to add the cheese, either the burger will be tough as luggage leather by the time it melts or the cheese will taste like a pack of playing cards when the grillman takes the burger off the grill. What does one do in this situation?

At that instant when in agony I've decided to say something—a big smile and, "Excuse me, I can't remember if I asked for that *cheeseburger medium rare?*"—the grillman miraculously discovers a square of American cheese at his fingertips. Like Doug Flutie lofting a football sixty yards into the end zone, he flings the cheese at the burger. It hits its target dead center, obviously bowing to some mysterious law of mutual attraction.

Occasionally a misguided grillman will place the cheese on the bun instead of the burger and brown it under the broiler. This is a crime in my book and probably warrants some form of community restitution. Cheese and burger must have time to get acquainted and to synergize in such a way that the cheese melts and runs down the side of the burger like lava down the slopes of Vesuvius.

Now all that remains is to worry that everything arrives at the same time—except the Coke, that is; it should get there early, to provide a diversion until the meal arrives. For some reason cheeseburgers definitely *do* go better with Coke. Perhaps it's because between bun and burger, fries, pickle, and slaw you're wedging so much food into your mouth at one time that only an industrial-strength soft drink can wash it all down and cleanse the palate for the next bite.

I take a quick glance along the counter to make sure the condiments are close at hand. There's nothing more maddening than realizing there's no mustard in sight after the grillman has delivered your meal and retreated to the parking lot to smoke a joint. I decline to express an opinion about the best condiments for burgers. In the same way that each cheeseburger is the grillman's masterpiece, condiments are the customer's contribution to the creative process and the expression of his individuality. If you want to dump a relish that looks and tastes like Chiclets on your burger, that's your business.

No burger joint is complete without a jukebox in every booth.

The only thing left to go wrong is the fries. Truth be told, if you really wanted the taste of a potato, you wouldn't order fries. Baked, mashed, or boiled, potatoes are frankly boring. But when peeled, sliced, and fried to crisp perfection, french fries fall into the category of confection. They are unassailable evidence that for all the ways man has found to foul his environment, he has also discovered a couple of ways to improve it.

The grillman has now set aside all other responsibilities and for the next several seconds will devote his dexterity to me and my burger. Lettuce, tomato, pickle, and cole slaw are arranged on the platter with the deliberation of a Cubist constructing collage. A bun, soft as a baby's bottom, is plucked from a plastic bag and pried open. In a single motion, the grillman slides his spatula beneath the still-sizzling burger, lifts it perilously into the air (I feel my cheek twitch and hear my heart murmur), and drops it into the open arms of the bun.

Finally the fries. Like treasure raised from the wreck of a Spanish galleon, my fries emerge from their oil golden and glistening and are emptied—absurdly generous quantities of them—onto every available millimeter of platter. Eyeing it with the slightest glint of self-satisfaction, the grillman places his creation before me and hurries away. I have no doubt that if the cheeseburger deluxe had been around in seventeenth-century Holland, the masters of the Dutch still life would have abandoned their frilly flower paintings for this composition most pleasing to the eye—the vibrant green and red of lettuce and tomato, the soothing circularity of the burger, the haphazard beauty of the fries.

Once my burger arrives, I never just plunge into it. I actually think about these things. It's only shyness that prevents me from going from person to person at the counter and showing them my burger, so proud of it am I. I can't help casting a pitying glance at all those sad-eyed secretaries sitting on the surrounding stools and picking at icy mounds of cottage cheese and canned cling peaches. I lift my burger—what other nutritionally balanced meal fits into the palm of your

The relationship between grill-man and customer is critical when a cheeseburger deluxe hangs in the balance.

hand?—and enjoy the pleasant sensation of its weight.

Burgers do have an optimal size—somewhere around five ounces. I feel no gratitude to those establishments that serve burgers the size of softballs that make the tendons in your jaw creak as you attempt to get your teeth around them. Also, burgers should never be cut in half like a grilled cheese sandwich. There is a joyous symmetry between bun and burger, and severing it is a crime against nature. How often have you bitten into a burger on one side and then taken your second bite 180 degrees from your first? Or taken any bite that was not contiguous to the previous one? One bows to the preordained order of things and experiences a simplehearted satisfaction watching the burger grow smaller and smaller. Who would deny that eating a cheeseburger is part ritual?

The fact that the fries often arrive boiling hot is both infuriating and invigorating—it makes you aware just how far you're willing to torture your tongue to experience the ecstasy of all those flavors and textures in your mouth at the same time. I plunge into my burger and momentarily lose consciousness. The entire universe will shrink to the size of my tastebuds. My method is to take a bite of my burger, a forkful of fries, and alternate the pickle and cole slaw. Show me a person who can finish his burger before starting his fries or who will devour his pickle in a single bite and I'll show you a person without self-control.

I remember the time I was having lunch with a girlfriend. I had perfectly alternated eating the elements of my cheeseburger deluxe so that what remained for my last bite was a modest but adequate morsel of burger and bun, six or seven fries, and a succulent nibble of pickle. I placed the burger in my mouth and added three or four fries. But as I was about to reach for the pickle, she grabbed it and popped it into her mouth. I broke up with her several seconds later, and though I still occasionally miss her company, I know I made the right decision.

by Russell Martin

One of these days Phil Donahue will do a show. I'll be the guy seen only in silhouette, my voice garbled to protect my true identity.

Phil will say, "Eugene—and of course that's not your real name—Eugene, you are here today to tell us that you are addicted to capsicum. You have been, for as long as you can remember, is that right? Under its influence, you have avoided Caesar salads for decades; you haven't had a swordfish fillet in donkey's years; you think that fresh pasta means macaroni and cheese eaten right out of the pan; you guess—am I right?—that a lamb curry is a brush for a sheep. Eugene, I think we all appreciate that this is going to be difficult for you, but if you would, could you speak to how in the world you got hooked on this stuff?"

Then I'll bare my soul. I'll confess that eating a burrito smothered in green chile with pozole and refritos on the side is my second favorite thing to do—and that my favorite thing to do always makes me hungry. I'll admit that I cannot drive by a café called Berta's or Trini's or Tranquilina's without stopping to eat. If the sign is hand-lettered and the beer posters are in Spanish, I will explain, I begin to get excited. If Trini herself is at work in the kitchen, and if her husband—Raúl or Rudy or Pete—is watching TV from a booth at the back, I know I'm in for a treat. I might even add—my electronically altered voice sounding as if I have been inhaling helium—that Mexican food seems to be damn near all there is to live for.

Fernando Armenta, owner of El Sol in Coos Bay, Oregon, isn't about to reveal the recipe for his homemade tamales.

The early diners were nothing more than railroad cars mounted on cinder blocks.

Before I get too carried away, Phil will interrupt me, and I suppose he'll explain for the uninitiated that capsicum isn't some vicious new controlled substance that is floated into the Florida swamps in fishing trawlers. No, it's just the name of the genus of fruits (belonging to the nightshade family) that bear large, multi-seeded pods tending toward the piquant end of the flavor spectrum; some varieties—the santaca, jalapeño, and Española, for instance—are frankly hotter than hell. Phil will have read up enough beforehand to know that although some people call them *peppers*, and although others forever misspell them as *chilis*, they are known throughout Latin America and the American Southwest as *chiles*. Better minds than Phil's or mine will have to explain why in the world they are fruits.

Before he breaks for a commercial, Phil will say, "I know we're long here, but I think it's important to make this point. Eugene is not an isolated case. There are thousands, hundreds of thousands of people in this country who share his addiction, whose lives have been radically altered by blue corn enchiladas and chiles relleños. And perhaps it's time we paid attention." Some of the women in the audience will gasp, muttering their shock to their neighbors. Others, of course, will just be bored by it all, checking the monitors to see if they can catch glimpses of themselves, wishing today's guest had been Tony Bennett.

When you come right down to it, you have to admit that this hemisphere is the home of some pretty terrific foodstuffs. Potatoes, tomatoes, the kernels-on-a-cob we call corn, and, of course, chiles.

Anthropologists digging in South America have found chile seeds that date from 700 B.C., but the genus is probably much older than that. The Mayans were eating hot chiles by 300 A.D., the Toltecs took to them in the 900s, and the Aztecs, who called them *axi*, were so impressed with them that by the 1400s they had accorded chiles the status of a minor deity.

In the late 1500s, the first Spanish explorers into the region that became New Mexico reported that the Pueblo peoples along the Rio

Preceding overleaf: The epitome of eclectic decorating at Romero's, in the tiny mining town of Silverton, Colorado.

Truckers are supposed to know where to find the best roadside food.

Grande were growing chiles in irrigated fields and were eating them in combination with cooked dried beans and a flat, unleavened bread made from corn—a staple that later became known as the tortilla.

Four hundred years later, the three—tortillas, beans, and chiles—remain the basic ingredients in a bi-national cuisine that is generically known as "Mexican." In Mexico, it is simply *comida*, or *comida del pueblo*; "Tex-Mex," though slightly derisive, is the preferred appellation in Texas. The victual variations that are native to northern New Mexico are sometimes distinguished by calling them *New* Mexican cooking. The simple phrase "Mexican food" is what you'll hear elsewhere—in the parts of Colorado, Arizona, and southern California where the real thing can sometimes be ferreted out.

The issue of what constitutes the real thing is one that has spawned much ill will and more than a few knife fights over the years. Can *real* tortillas be made out of wheat flour as well as *masa*, corn meal? (Yes.) Can *real* sopaipillas be a heavy, grease-drenched, cinnamon-sprinkled dessert pastry as well as a light, airy, nearly angelic bread that accompanies the main course? (No!) Is green chile hotter than red? (It depends.) Do you make tacos by rolling the tortillas up like a scroll or by folding them in half like an envelope? (It . . . still depends.)

I suppose the reason why there is so much difference of opinion about how Mexican food should be prepared is that the cuisine is indigenous to such an enormous reach of this continent. Many people—fools and neophytes that they are—assume that any Mexican food served in the United States is a pale and peculiar bastardization of the *real* stuff that is native to the Mexican republic. Well, the truth is that Hispanic settlers moved into the areas surrounding Taos, Tucson, and San Diego almost as early as they did to Tuxpan, Tecomán, and San Miguel de Allende. The cuisine they created in both the north and the south borrowed heavily from the cooking that was already established in those places—the food that belonged to the native Indian inhabitants. The evolution of this new, now-Hispanic cuisine over the succeeding centuries made use of local ingredients and local preferences. But none of them were imposters, none represented the true

Self-congratulation is always a good sign.

and catholic way to cook, and that is why the enchiladas suizas served at Mi Tierra in San Antonio are just as wondrous and *authentic* as those they dazzle you with at Las Cazuelas in Mexico City.

Here is the harsh reality, however. Just because you recognize that Mexican cooking encompasses great variety, you cannot, you *must* not, assume that all the Mexican food you will encounter during your aimless Southwestern tours in that cruise-controlled Oldsmobile will be memorable. That kind of naïveté could get you into a heap of trouble. The chances of finding a meal that will leave you feeling like your sins have been forgiven have significantly diminished in recent years because of two disturbing new phenomena. The first is the fast-food Mexican joint where they throw any damn thing they can think of between a wretched pre-formed tortilla, call it the something-or-other-*ito*, and serve it with a side of "Mexi-fries"—french fries sprinkled with chile molido. Shocking though it seems to me, these people appear to be breaking no local laws.

Equally worrisome is the second trend, illustrated by the spate of "quality" franchised Mexican restaurants, usually located in shopping centers, the sorts of places where they spend six million dollars on Mexican tile, stuccoed archways, and open-air patios, then hire high school football players as cooks. The food at these places is uniformly uninteresting, but the one thing they have somehow gotten a handle on is the noble margarita. If you realize you're in suspicious surroundings, here's what I recommend: Order a pitcher of margaritas, eat the tortilla chips and salsa (which will be called "our complimentary spicy Mexican dip"), then go get in line at Wendy's.

But let's say you're driving from Brownsville to Bakersfield, or from Denver to San Bernardino, and you'd like to have five or six good meals along the way. How can you find the places that hold great gastronomic promise? Well, if you think I'm going to make a list of all the great Southwestern cafés I've run into after years of obsessive chile-eating, then your hat's too tight. Sure, I'll mention a couple of them, but if I told you where the best ones were, then you'd tell your

A meal at Patricio's Café in Manzanola, Colorado, is a delicious antidote to the loneliness of the long-distance driver.

friends to be sure and check them out, and before long we'd all have to wait forty-five minutes to get a table, and the nice families that run these restaurants would be tempted to build big additions and to do them all up in Don Quixote motifs. You see the problem.

But there are a few rules of thumb that I can safely pass along, a few trustworthy things to look for.

Location. This is fundamental. You will never find a decent Mexican restaurant at an Interstate Highway interchange; I think it's some sort of federal regulation. The best Mexican restaurants are located downtown in small towns, on the south side of big towns, and on the edge of little, patchy, shoulderless highways—in that order. Genero's in Gallup, New Mexico, is one of the few good Mexican cafés I can think of that are anywhere near an Interstate. It lies about a half mile south of I-40 itself, and only a couple of blocks below the I-40 busi-

A still-life of spirits glows in the late-afternoon sunlight.

ness loop, which used to be called Route 66 back in the days when we wrote songs and made TV series out of a stretch of highway. But the vast majority of Genero's patrons never get on the Interstate anyway, except maybe to drive out to the Union 76 truck stop once a week to buy cheap gas. Most of them live right in Gallup proper, or out on the Navajo or Zuni reservations. They come to Genero's five days a week, eleven to ten, to sit and eat in its dark, cavernous confines, which resemble nothing so much as the parish hall of a poor church where the shades have been drawn to show a movie about the Holy Land. Genero's food is truly incendiary; people drink four Cokes or three beers just to get themselves through their meals, and it is probably just as well that none of them is heading for Flagstaff after supper.

Name. Never eat in a Mexican restaurant that is named after a conquistador, an animal, or a local rock that resembles either of the two.

If it is called La Buena Vida, The Good Life, it might be a good choice; if it is call La Cocina, The Kitchen, it is probably a sensible enough establishment. But your best bet is probably a place that simply bears its owner's name—first, last, or both. Female first names tend to predominate in this category for reasons that may seem obvious. An Albuquerque eatery of cultish renown was first known simply as Ron y Marcia, the names of the young couple who operated it. But when Marcia ran off with a customer, Ron, with what has to be considered an impressive stoic resolve, simply changed the name to Ron *Sin* Marcia. He didn't want to mislead anyone.

Decor. As a general rule, if a restaurant is carpeted, it's a bad sign. If it has fabric tablecloths, it is a very bad sign, although vinyl tablecloths should pose no problem. Be suspicious of candles in amber fish bowls, silverware of a single design, and waitresses who are dressed in uniforms that make them resemble Hungarian peasants. Parrots or canaries in cages, paintings on black velvet with religious or amorous themes, jukeboxes that are filled with the latest Mexican polkas, and paper placemats with inaccurate maps of the state supplied by Coors beer are all very good signs.

In Santa Fe, at one of the world's great Mexican cafés—whose name I just don't happen to remember—three rows of white wooden booths are crowded into a space narrower by half than the body of a 747. Daily specials are scribbled with Magic Marker on white paper bags that are taped to one of the walls. Dominating the opposite wall is a large, realistic painting of the proprietress herself—whose name I still can't remember—standing serenely in her six-by-seven-foot kitchen.

Owners and employees. It is not necessarily a bad sign if the person waiting on you looks like she is Scandinavian; it may even be okay if the person waiting on you is male. But for some reason, most men in the better Mexican cafés tend to do nothing but operate the cash register. If the restaurant is obviously a family operation, you had better sit down and eat. At Garcia's on Fourth Street in Albuquerque (not to be confused with Garcia's of Scottsdale, one of the aforementioned fancy

Customers at Chili Willi's in Huntington, West Virginia, roll up their sleeves and dig in.

franchises), photos of three generations of the Garcia family fill every available vertical space. Baby pictures, high school graduation portraits, and snapshots of the family's trips to Hawaii are right there for everyone to peruse and enjoy. The waitresses at Garcia's, some of them Hispanic and others Anglo, greet their regular breakfast customers with cups of hot coffee and know they want carne adovada and eggs without even having to ask.

Menu. This one is tricky. It is sometimes a good sign if the menu, set in small type, fills four or five pages. At other establishments, it is a good sign if the complete menu is seven items scribbled in faint chalk on a blackboard. Beware of restaurants that seem to specialize in combination plates; combination plates were invented by some substandard restaurateur who figured that if he jumbled five or six entrées together on a large platter, you wouldn't realize that none of them was worth spending your Saturday-night money on. It never hurts to ask the waitress what the café's most popular dish is; a truly distinguished *comedor* always prepares some things better than others. When you go to Houston's Cadillac Bar, of course, you eat cabrito—braised goat—while you read the walls, so covered with graffiti they make New York's IRT trains look like they're brand new. At The Shed in Santa Fe, where you duck under five-foot door jambs to get to your table, you wave off the other options and go straight for the blue corn enchiladas covered with a red chile that may well be the source of life on earth. At Vallejo's on south Corona Street in Colorado Springs, where the parrot motif reaches its zenith, and where the TV is always turned toward the kitchen's serving window, you always eat tamales. You wouldn't think of doing otherwise.

Any Mexican restaurant with a wine list is a place to be pitied; next year at this time it will no doubt be a Burger Heaven. There are only two acceptable beverages to drink with Mexican food, whether served in this country or in Mexico. One is Coke—*old* Coke, of course. The other, and the preferred, is beer, served in pitchers or longnecked bottles. It has become fashionable for even the most modest cafés to serve Mexican beers with colored foil on the necks of the bottles.

The first foray into this combination platter could send red beans and rice over the edge.

Many Mexican beers deserve their rich reputations, but I am often tempted to drink the regular old American swill when I remember that in restaurants in Mexico, where they forgo the foil, you can drink them for a third the price.

I recently read something that has me worried. It was a piece by journalist Alexander Cockburn about a new restaurant in Manhattan Beach, California (which tells you something already), that serves a sort of food called *nouvelle* New Mexican cuisine. Located in the Manhattan Village Mall, the Saint Estephe has a menu that begins with a short story—this one historical, all about the first American civilizations—then lists items that include seabass tamales, "New Mexican-style raviolis," and even blue corn tortillas "served with smoked salmon and two types of American caviar," for crying out loud. Fresh prawns from Arizona flavored with nopalitos are also touted. Have you been to Arizona? Where do they find these prawns? In the swimming pools in Scottsdale?

Now, the Saint Estephe may become a big hit. The way things are going in America these days, I wouldn't doubt it. The guys who run it might even make Donahue. But up until now, Mexican food has mercifully escaped the attention of the cuisine-as-social-statement crowd. First it happened with fish; then Cajun cooking caught their eyes. I'm worried that Mexican fare won't be far behind. But, maybe I'm making too much of this development. The Saint Estephe may already be so *nouvelle* that any real anchor in the Mexican tradition is hard to identify. My hunch is that you would have a hard time finding anything on the menu with enough chile in it to make your nostrils steam and your brow break out in a sweat. I would guess that if you asked your waiter for a big side of refritos to go with your Arizona prawns, he would look slightly aghast. I'll bet there isn't a parrot in the place.

Overleaf: Chuck's Place in Avondale, Colorado, dispenses good cheer.

LOBSTER

Greetings From MAINE

State Capitol in Augusta

State Flower
the Pine Cone and Tassel

Enjoying a Dip

by LeRoy Woodson, Jr.

It was fall when I embarked on the first leg of what would become a 20,000-mile journey across America. I was setting out to look for food. I wanted to photograph restaurants, roadhouses, cafés, diners, shacks—the eccentric out-of-the-way places that serve home-cooked food the old-fashioned way. I knew these places were probably still around, hiding somewhere off the main road. I also knew the kind of people I'd be looking for. They'd be good, down-to-earth people who cared about their customers. Folks who spared no effort in their uncompromising search for the best quality. Cooks who wanted to see their customers satisfied and well fed. I was bound to discover these places and these people.

Since it was fall, I thought I'd start by heading off for Maine; it was a great opportunity to drive through a landscape of rich color. The day I left was warm, and New York City was starting to wake up as I finished packing my car in the shadow of the Singer building on lower Broadway. By the time I hit the road, traffic was heavy. Simply leaving the city was turning into a chore. Nevertheless, a spirit of high adventure prevailed. And it wasn't long before city traffic fell behind and I started to get into the rhythm of the trip.

Traveling alone in a little orange car—with the sounds of the engine and the wind and the traffic—imposes a degree of solitude not found anywhere else. This gave me the time, almost the inclination, to take a deep breath and appreciate the brilliance of New England's fall foliage. It also gave me time to think. I started to remember trips I

Bibs and beer are basics for a lobster lunch at Nunan's Lobster Hut in Cape Porpoise, Maine.

Above: At Hancock's Lobster Pound in Ogunquit, Maine, each lobster is weighed, stuffed into a string bag, and cooked—bag and all—in sea water.

had taken with my family when I was young. We were never sure we'd find a place to eat, so the car was always packed with a big lunch of fried chicken and potato salad. This time the car was packed with cameras.

I passed a lot of roadside pits along the way. They all had an impersonal look about them, more rushed than anything else. This was the kind of place I wanted to avoid. If nothing else, they just didn't look welcoming. An image that kept popping up was that character Ben from *The Last Picture Show*, the guy who served cheeseburgers and milkshakes and advice to the town's teenagers. In a small town there are no secrets, and it's almost as if the restaurant and its owners are a second home. Proprietors end up becoming temporary caretakers for the kids, offering not only food for the stomach but support or advice or just an ear—food for the soul. I didn't think I'd find a Ben at any of these places.

The sun was shining brightly as I came upon the "Welcome to Maine" sign. I crossed the Piscataqua and headed for Route 1, the coastal highway. Sure, I had done some research about where I should look for roadside places, but in the end it seemed that the best bet would be to nose places out, to be persuaded by the decor, the promises of innocent-looking signs, word of mouth, even the beauty of the surroundings.

One place that had sounded good at first was Hancock's Lobster Pound in Ogunquit. The first time I had heard the name I had chuckled to myself—the image that came to mind had been of dog pounds, and I wondered if I might come across a penned-in area filled with yapping lobsters. When I got there I was sure I'd found the right kind of place. Hancock's is an elegant lodge made of cedar logs and white pine, set in a glorious stand of pine trees. There were picnic tables and graveled walks under the looming fifty-foot pines, and as I approached the lodge I felt like I was entering a small forest. Next to the lodge was the pound. No yapping lobsters behind fences, but two large tanks filled with sea water that's run up from the ocean by a

1,000-foot pipeline. Live lobsters, their claws locked open with small wooden spikes, scuttled around the tank—trying desperately to hide, struggling to be as inconspicuous as possible. There were also clams in the tank. The clams just sat there.

The first bit of information I uncovered was that Bill Hancock and his sister Lisa had just taken over the operation from their grandmother, Hazel Hancock, and that the Pound had a long, happy history in the area. Customers have been coming back for over thirty years, bringing their children and grandchildren for spectacular food. This is good, old-time, home-cooked food. The pies—deep-dish blueberry and apple—are still made from Hazel Hancock's recipes, the same ones that have been used since 1944; and until she took charge of the staff, Lisa made all the pies herself.

Bill Hancock oversees the whole operation, and at times he seems more like a father trying to put food on the table for his family—only this family consumes between six and eight hundred pounds of lobster a week. And when the lobster fishermen are having a run of poor catches, Bill worries. "Sometimes I wake up on a Sunday morning, not knowing if there're going to be enough lobsters for business."

A lobsterman confronts his catch.

Don Neil, though, never seems to worry. Don presides over the tanks and boiling pots. The ritual is for customers to select their own lobsters. Don—a big, imposing man with close-cropped hair and a bright yellow apron—used to be a marine; and he runs this line with boot camp efficiency. You stay in line (Don's glance can be withering to the upstart who tries to cut in on a busy night) until it's your turn to pick. Then Don will weigh your lobster and stuff it into a string sack. The lobster, sack and all, gets dropped into the boiling lobster pot, and a string from the bag is wrapped around a nail labeled with the order number.

Once the lobster's done, it's pulled from the pot, with a dramatic eruption of steam, and dipped into cold water to cool it enough for the kids on the staff to clean it. One cleaner will snap the body open in half with a quick whack of a knife; another will crack the claws and put the cleaned lobster into a paper boat for serving.

When it was my turn to select a lobster, I ordered a three-pound one. After glorying behind my plastic bib in the lobster and clarified butter and baked beans and cole slaw and salad, I still had room for a piece of pie. What a meal, from the rich mellowness of the lobster and butter to the tang of the tiny wild blueberries. Finding Hancock's was a perfect beginning for my trip.

I made another early start the next day. It was probably the sharp, clean sea air that got me out of bed. I followed the coast, ducking in and out of tiny seaports—stopping once or twice to take a picture—until I came upon Cape Porpoise.

Just down the street from the docks was a rather weatherbeaten shack painted in bright reds and yellows. This was Nunan's Lobster Hut, and there was something inviting about it. I went up and looked in the windows. There were tables and benches painted battleship gray, and everything looked spotlessly clean. Wooden shutters lined the walls, tied back with pieces of heavy rope wrapped around stays, and the ceiling and walls were covered with years and years of memorabilia, including a giant lobster (caught, I later learned, in the nineteenth century by great-grandfather Nunan).

The door to the kitchen is right near the customers' entrance, and I stuck my nose in to find Clara Hutchins picking lobster claws. I told her what I was up to and she dropped her claw and said I'd better meet Bertha right away. She just wanted a second to wipe off her hands and she'd take me over.

Bertha Nunan—a tall, grandmotherly lady with a ready wit and an impish smile behind metal-framed glasses—was in her kitchen, finishing her baking, and she sat me down in her cluttered kitchen with a cup of coffee. There was a flurry of activity. "I have to go check on ma pies. I can't smell 'em . . . Immune to 'em, you know. You get immune to 'em after a while. I can't smell lobsters either. People say, 'Oh, those lobsters smell good!' She laughed. "I can't smell either."

Whether she can smell them or not, the pies are legendary—especially the blueberry pies. When the season hits its peak, Bertha will make forty blueberry pies, eight or ten apple pies, and some brownies and biscuits each morning.

For plain speaking and straight-ahead friendliness, Bertha Nunan is hard to beat. She's been the sole owner of the Lobster Hut since her

Lobster fishermen check their traps.

husband passed away in 1974. She told me that her father-in-law had started the business in '53, that there was just one small section then. Now, Nunan's seats 124 in the dining room, and they serve only lobster and clams. Yes, she has help, her sons Keith and Richard. She seems to appreciate the importance of tradition, of continuity. (She's been baking in the same oven for twenty years.) It was a good thing I'd come when I did, she told me, because she was getting ready to close up for the season. She invited me to come back for the annual closing party, her gift to the staff.

I came back early that night, to watch the goings-on in the kitchen. As I came in the kitchen door, the first thing I saw was the seven kettles lined up on burners with fiercely burning flames. Bertha starts each order fresh with two inches of water in the kettle, and the juices of the lobsters combine with the water to make a fragrant, steaming broth that cooks the lobsters. It's always two inches of water, whether one lobster goes into the pot or eight, and they come out perfect each time. Bertha cooks chicks (the one-pound lobsters) for twenty minutes. The heffers (pound-and-a-halfers) take twenty-five minutes; the quarters (one-and-a-quarter pounds) take less time than the heffers, but more than the chicks.

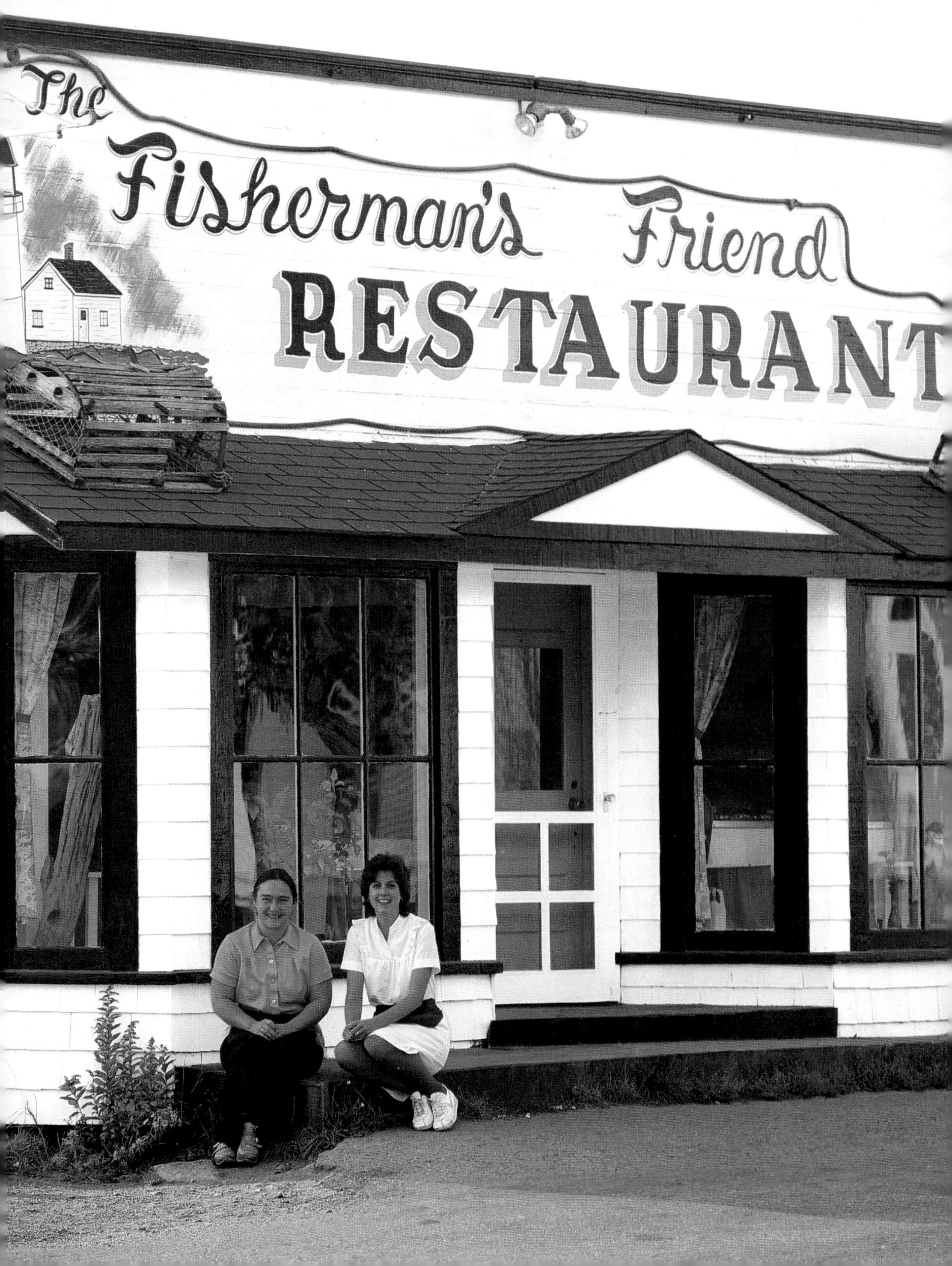
The Fisherman's Friend
RESTAURANT

The bustle in the kitchen finally began to slow down. Bertha was sitting at the table, with her eye on the clock and two kettles at the same time. The few remaining customers were vying with each other for the honor of being the last served of the season. Bertha's son Richard wandered in, then Keith and his girlfriend. I was aware of a feeling of real anticipation in the air.

Finally it was all over. As the last customers filed out of the Lobster Hut, cheers were sounded all around. Bottles of beer and wine appeared, and the waitresses scurried around laughing and joking and cleaning up for the party. In the kitchen, Herbert Hutchins began filling the kettles with the first of the party lobsters. Once these were done, he dumped them out at the cleaning station and started on the second run. Richard, long acknowledged as Nunan's fastest man with a knife, began splitting tails and cracking claws and tossing cleaned lobsters onto trays. The waitresses ran the heaping trays out to the dining room, tied on plastic bibs, and dug in. Kettle after kettle of lobsters were cooked and cleaned, and we all kept on eating. Then, once I was sure no human stomach could hold another morsel, giant slabs of Bertha's blueberry pie with tennis balls of vanilla ice cream appeared. We protested, but we dug in once more. Stuffed, and not entirely sober, we finally dispersed amid tears and warm embraces, bidding each other good luck—even Merry Christmas and Happy New Year, months in advance.

The next morning I was off again. My journey eventually took me south through the gentle hills of Virginia and the elegance of the cypress swamps of the Cajun bayous. I drove through the awe-inspiring mountains of the Continental Divide past the splendors of the Pacific Ocean coast and the staggering beauty of the northwest's redwood forests. All the time I was looking for the quintessentially American food experience. Sometimes I found it; other times I was disappointed. But throughout the trip I kept the memory of those first few days—the beauty of the weather, the warmth and generosity of the welcome, and the simple goodness of the food.

Unfailing good cheer at the Fisherman's Friend in Stonington, Maine.

HOT DOGS

by Timothy White

Throughout history, we've all been fed a lot of quasi-meaty hoodoo about the enduring Germanic grandeur of the frankfurter, the medieval invention named for the ancient port city of Frankfurt. Frankly, hot dogs have always been Greek to me, and reached their apex, in my toothsome estimation, in the output of two family-owned chains that humbly sizzle and satisfy within twenty minutes of the George Washington Bridge. Of all the mobile meals created since antiquity (manna, pemmican, Mars bars), I don't think any rival the tongue-scalding superiority of a well-turned wiener in a toasted bun—that is, a bun whose sides are just high enough to contain a hearty slather of mustard and sauerkraut while you're trying to hold onto the wheel.

My late father was already renowned as a peerless one-armed hot-dog chomper when he introduced me as a five-year-old to Teddy's in Paterson, New Jersey, and Papaya King in New York City. Guiding the family's wheezing, pea-green '53 Ford Custom wagon into the cramped parking lot of Teddy's or to the grimy curb at the Papaya King stand on 86th Street and Third Avenue, Dad was always boisterous in his ritual declaration that a good hot dog, rather than being ideal ball park fare, was actually best consumed in the comfort of the car—preferably with the motor running.

While the term "hot dog" was coined in 1901 at the New York Polo Grounds by cartoonist Tod Dorgan, with a playful caricature of the "dachshund sausages" that had been hawked at Coney Island since

Roadside food New York City style. (Michelle Siegel)

1871, it took Constantine "Gus" Poulos, a native of the Greek town of Smyrna, to cook up a tube steak that, as his motto attests, is "tastier than filet mignon." The long, slender, impeccably spiced weiner is the product of Papaya King, a four-store Manhattan concern that also features milkshake-sized cups of the peculiarly compatible fruit juice. The flagship store has been located on the corner of 86th Street and Third Avenue since the 1930s, when it had various bland names like Hawaiian Fruit Drinks. But it became the fast-food eatery of choice for discriminating doggers in the mid-1950s, when Gus re-christened the business Papaya King and created its low-rent Disney logo, a smiling oval *Carica papaya* personification topped with a jaunty coronet.

Arriving in New York at the age of sixteen, fleeing the World War I occupation of the Turks (who had seized his family's prosperous food export concern), Gus Poulos got a job as a counter boy in a deli, and within two years he'd bought the business from his boss when the guy retired. After a decade or so Gus unloaded it himself and went into the gift candy business. Next came a string of popcorn concessions in amusement parks in the metropolitan area. All the while, the raffish young bachelor had been tripping down to Miami on sportive vacations and had grown quite fond of the exotic tropical fruits and juices available in sun-splashed Florida. He shipped up cases of locally grown papayas and sold juice and fancy baskets of other assorted fruits in the 86th Street stand, which he rigged up to look like a cross between a health bar and Tarzan's favorite rest stop. Women in grass skirts gave out free samples on the sidewalk while the loquacious Gus touted its nutritious and salubrious properties. The German immigrant population of Yorkville was not overwhelmed by the odd libation, however, whose mildly tart taste was reminiscent of a melted Creamsicle. As a hedge, Gus added a window where suspicious passersby could be hooked with smoked franks. At first, the German-Americans preferred to eat the hot weiners minus the toasted bun (buns were first introduced at St. Louis's 1904 Louisiana Purchase

Exposition), but gradually they bought the whole package, blond beverage and all.

When I was a kid, Papaya King drew its share of Bobbiesoxers, motorcycle toughs, and timid nobodies in gray flannel suits, but these days the trade regularly includes sportscaster Howard Cosell, who comes by on Saturdays in his limousine, and Woody Allen, who shot scenes for his film *Manhattan* in the sister store at 87th and Third. Every Friday evening a businessman based in Washington, D.C., buys ten pounds of the franks (which are made expressly for Papaya King by a butchery whose name the Poulos family will not disclose), and mail orders from Ireland, France, and England are routinely processed.

Sustenance for the soul, at Papaya King. (Leslie Lee)

On an average day, some three thousand hot dogs-cum-papaya-squeezings are briskly dispensed to movie stars, stock brokers, on-duty cops, and other assorted New Yorkers from the 86th Street grill alone. It's a loyal crew, too. In the late 1970s a franchise of the famed Nathan's hot dog dynasty opened an outlet next to the 86th Street store and vowed to "bury" it in a challenge the local newspapers dubbed the "Hot Dog Wars." Within a year, Nathan's was gone.

It takes a cool head to grill a great hot dog, and Gus and his dapper son Peter, a business school graduate who was born in the neighborhood, have mastered the art of the well-tempered wurst.

"Our franks are 100 percent premium beef with no fillers or by-products of any kind," says forty-seven-year-old Peter Poulos, a

Hot dogs and papaya juice—who could ask for anything more? (Leslie Lee)

handsome, silver-haired former investment banker (he hated the "stiffs" in the profession). Dressed in a tailored blue blazer and tan slacks, he stands behind the counter of the main branch, and with reflex tenderness, lifts a dog off the grill with the use of a long, doughy bun and heaps it high with sauerkraut.

"We have a nice toasted bun here," he declares with a paternal coo. "We have the finest grade of sauerkraut and"—reaching for a dollop of the condiment—"a special blend of Dijon mustard."

But the key is the kind of heat applied to the frank. "You must cook on a gas grill, because an electric grill can't balance the heat. We cannot have a mushy dog. It's gotta have that tight *give* when you bite into it."

Each time I subject a Papaya King dog to oral scrutiny, the application of my incisors triggers a *snap!* so resonant it would assure a blind man that he was dining on the genuine article. The meat is firm and explodes with a tangy torrent of somewhat peppery juice that fairly assaults my gums, and produces an immediate impulse to preserve the savory, nearly religious sensation. It is at this juncture that the grinning grillman always produces the tall cup of papaya nectar (regardless of how you place your order, the juice always shows up midway into the first frank), and as I drink deeply from the (thankfully unwaxy) cup I am amazed at how the custardy juice enhances the dog. There is a mild impression of room spin, and then I am consumed with the will to consume.

After (always) ordering two more dogs, my eye ambles involuntarily through the forest of garish signs that have always crowded the walls: "PAPAYA: THE DRINK OF ANGELS"—Christopher Columbus; "WE DEFY YOU TO FIND ANOTHER ESTABLISHMENT IN NYC WHERE YOU CAN GET FASTER AND BETTER SERVICE"; "THIS ESTABLISHMENT IS UNDER THE MANAGEMENT OF GUS POULOS. FOR ALL COMPLAINTS OR CONSTRUCTIVE CRITICISM WRITE TO GUS POULOS C/O PAPAYA KING, 179 EAST 86TH STREET 10028." There is also a large arrangement of mounted color photos of father and son inspecting a crop of fruit under the glowing palms, with the legend, "We found a *richer* papaya in Hawaii!"

"We don't get our papayas from Florida anymore," says Peter. "They couldn't keep the standards up. I've gone to Jamaica, the Bahamas, and Mexico for the best harvests, but ultimately none of them could meet our demands. We've gone as far as India looking for premium fruit, but Hawaii's got the best grade because of the volcanic soil. We have to have complete control of our fruit and our franks or the whole thing falls apart."

Still, there are those willing to surrender a measure of hot dog methodology in quest of a higher aesthetic—a mighty topping. At Teddy's, the ageless luncheonette on Market Street in Paterson, New Jersey, Theodore Constandelis always let the Schickhaus Frankfurter Company handle the raw material while he fretted over the fine tuning.

A native of the Greek island of Lemnos who arrived in this country around 1920, Constandelis dabbled in various businesses before joining with partners Charles Caravoulias and Peter Pappas to open Teddy's in 1954. Pappas had a recipe for a kind of chili sauce that Constandelis and Caravoulias thought had uncommon allure, and after additional tinkering, which involved adding unspecified amounts of paprika and cumin, they felt themselves prepared for the wurst. Whereas the Papaya King code decrees that a frank's surface must be as sleek and brightly scarlet as culinary science will allow, Teddy's aims for an appealingly terra-cotta tube with a wrinkled complexion—the better to hold the sauce. To this end, the franks are deep-fried in fresh vegetable shortening and then smothered with the heated, piquant finale, which also includes fresh onions and sharp mustard.

Since day one, the sensual experience of two Teddy's all-the-way has been complemented by a spiky heap of french fries, an addition that also contradicts the spare-minded "don't confuse the meal" creed of Papaya King. Teddy's potatoes are all direct-from-the-sack Idaho spuds which are hand peeled, blanched, and then deep fried in clear vegetable shortening for four to five minutes. Then they are stored in a walk-in freezer in the basement until the following day, when they are

Overleaf: The beverage of choice to accompany a couple of spicy franks at New York's Papaya King is fresh papaya juice, "the drink of angels." Although originally the papayas were supplied from the Florida crop, today the fruit comes from Hawaii.

DRINK PAPAYA & Stay Healthy

Perfectly Ripe
Chiquita
Bananas

Make Our
Banana Dace

Nobody, But Nobody Can
A Better 100% All Natu

PAPAYA

Because it is the Real McCoy made f
melon from the tropics, No artificial flavor
Enjoy a cup NOW & DISCOVER THIS W

Reg
8oz 60¢ | Med
16 oz
Twice
As Much

e in 30 oz. Contain

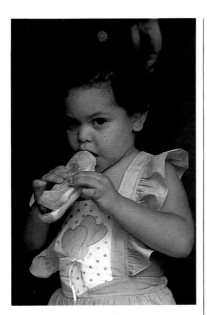

A young customer joins Papaya King's legion of fans. (Leslie Lee)

quick-fried once more and served to those who appreciate a sublimely unsoggy crispness in a fry. Silverware consists of a single skinny wooden cocktail fork, and the whole steaming repast is always served on an off-white paper platter that feels like starched chamois.

For more than thirty years, the hot-pink beacon that is Teddy's sign has been a source of uplift for numberless local politicians and luminaries in the tri-state area, as well as the young citizens of Paterson. I remember many a night in the summer of 1959, pulling up with my older brother Doug in his black '49 Chevy torpedo-back bomber and ordering several dogs, which we would balance in a row on the red, white, and blue pinstripe-covered dashboard. We ate at a wicked pace; "Don't worry," went the usual line, "you're gonna be tastin' this meal for *days*." And we listened to the Drifters' "There Goes My Baby" and "Come Softly to Me" by the Fleetwoods, the music oozing from two stolen drive-in movie speakers Doug had wired to the radio to produce triophonic sound.

All the guys ate in their machines, for that matter, and on any given evening in the late 1950s the parking lot hummed and roared with a fender-to-fender phalanx of hot rods filled with ducktailed delinquents from East Side High, St. Joe's, and St. John's, each passenger with one eye on the food and the other on the jailbait in poodle dresses and saddle shoes who streamed along the sidewalk.

Weekends, the lot is still virtually impregnable to pedestrians, and wobbly bar chairs have been stuck between the old chrome stools to increase the counter seating, but the view from the front window and the windshield has evolved from a landscape of sweet young things to one of small bands of panhandling breakdancers spinning on flattened refrigerator cartons.

"At one point we got so overwhelmed with business and the demand for the sauce alone became so great that we had the Venice Maid Company of Vineland, New Jersey, selling it in a can," says the jolly, sixty-four-year-old Nick Constandelis, who now shoulders most of his dad's former responsibilities—including flirting with the coquettish young waitresses. "But after a while we discontinued that because it became a distribution bother and the can perhaps changed the flavor a bit. So now we sell a dried version on the premises; you add water at home and it's *almost* as good. I make two sixty-gallon drums of the sauce every morning; if you want the absolute best, you gotta come to the source."

Damn straight. But it's worth the drive for another reason: Teddy's is one of the last bastions of vintage diner argot. None of the employees in the little white stone building can relay an order to the kitchen in an idiom other than undiluted beanery-ese: "Hey, draw a deuce (two coffees) and give me one away one (a dog with everything on it)!!"

Like Teddy Constandelis, his other partners are now retired, and any further expansion of the concern will remain under the family umbrella. Nick's brother Peter has been managing a Teddy's out on Route 23 in Butler, New Jersey, for five years, and "people say his sauce is identical to mine," Nick insists.

As for the pilots of Papaya King, Peter Poulos says that their dream is to open an outlet in London, his favorite city in the world. But he's wary. "I have to be able to sell the same American beef product from our butcher, and that's a lot of red tape." For the time being, Poulos has his hands full seven days a week running the four Manhattan stores, especially the bustling Papaya King on Nassau Street in the financial district and the newest addition, on the corner of 59th Street and Third Avenue.

"When we took over the establishment on 59th Street, it was a Greek gyro place that also did a good trade in pizza," Nick confides. "Of course, I didn't want the gyro stuff or any of the rest of the former menu, and the store was completely redesigned with our bright tropical decor and my dad's corny but catchy signs. Thing was, the place sold so much pizza that I decided to rebuild the shop so that it was two distinctly separate restaurants under one roof."

He shrugs. "I mean, I just couldn't picture people eating pizza with papaya juice."

RIBS

by J. C. Suarès

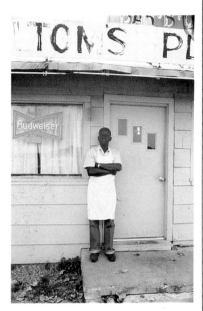

Above and opposite: Alonzo "Slick" Smith poses in front of the restaurant that bears his name (sort of) in Muskogee, Oklahoma. (J. C. Suarès)

Overleaf: Sandwiches are only available for another hour and fifty-seven minutes, but you can get ribs any time. (J. C. Suarès)

The sign on the gray cinderblock shack on Oklahoma's Highway 62 reads STLOM, and if you didn't know to look for the rigs and Cadillacs, you'd be smack in the middle of Muskogee before you realized you missed Slick's altogether. Slick doesn't believe in fancy signs; not that he didn't try, but that was a long time ago, when he first moved in.

Here's the story. When Slick came here in 1959, the place had been Tom's. Slick covered Tom's name above the door with a coat of white paint borrowed from a nearby lot (and quickly returned). Next he asked a friend to letter SLICK over it with black paint. The large black letters looked very professional from Sunday afternoon until the following Thursday. That morning a bunch of burly black clouds from Texas crashed into each other in a free-for-all above Muskogee, sending down two inches of rain in twenty minutes on Slick's new sign. The borrowed paint was not water-resistant and the sign ran, melting the I, the C, and the K. Slick never bothered to fix the problem, and if you knew him you'd understand why. He's a curt and impatient type who is not partial to ceremony or small talk. He only cares about cooking the best ribs in Oklahoma, and he never thinks twice about silly things like printing up menus (a blackboard will do), or serving food on plates (it's served on wax paper), or having a pretty sign above the door. Anyway, Slick is so well known around these parts that a sign is hardly necessary. Jim Leake, the richest man in Muskogee

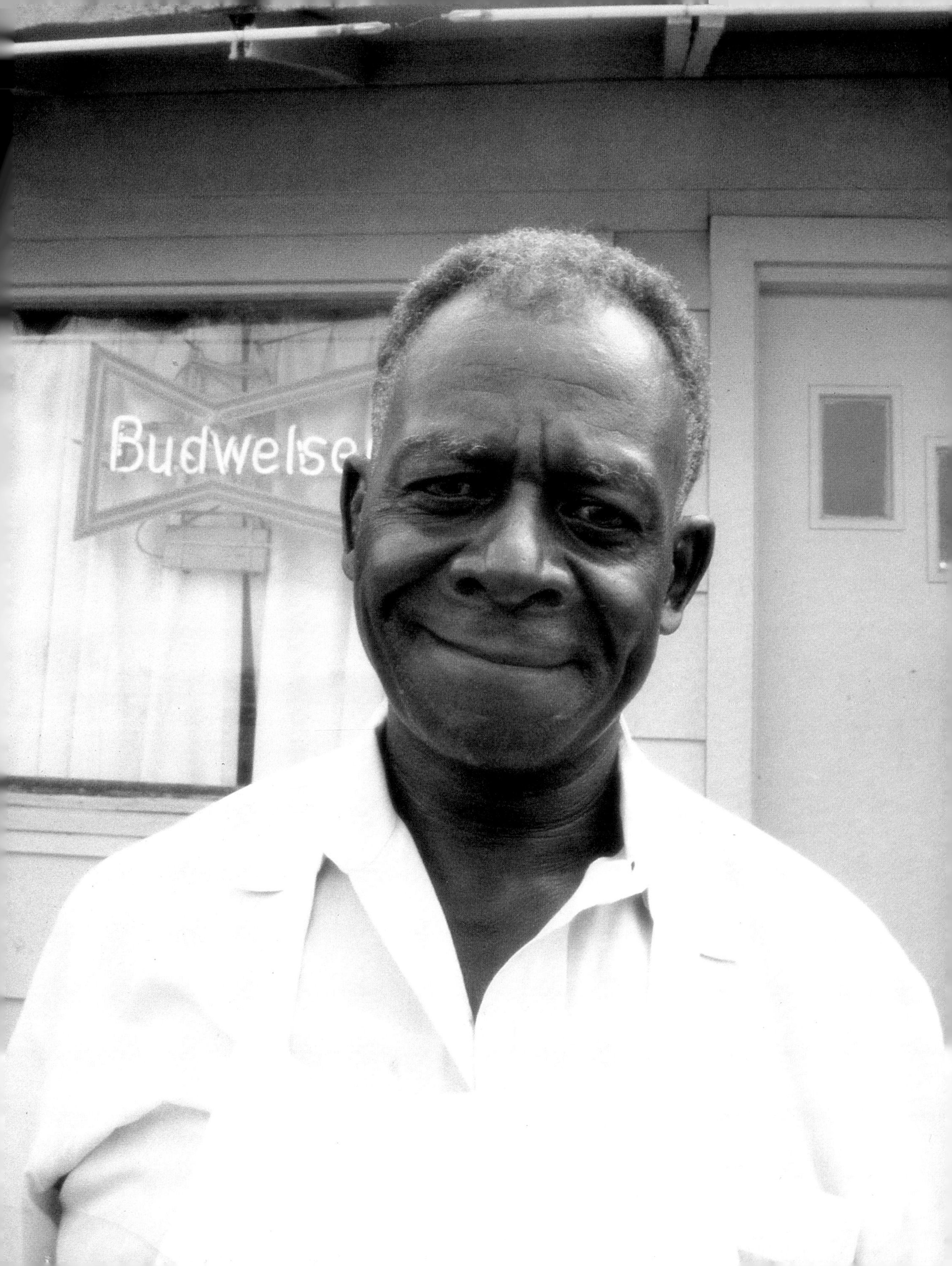
Budweise

RE PLACE
FOR LESS"
ACROSS STREET
ARKET
rown Porter Peaches
LIVE FISH BAIT
S PRODUCE
Fresh FRUIT and VEGETABLES
KING
KAN
"IS HERE"
Miller
ES SERVED AFTER 4: PM
FRIDAY'S
CLOCK WED.
AY
SLICK

and Slick's landlord, was surprised that they hadn't heard of Slick's restaurant in Manhattan. He insisted I drive there for lunch.

As I was to find out, everybody eats at Slick's. Three hundred people a day come from as far away as Texas: There are Creek Indians with long black ponytails, farmers in blue faded overalls, truckers in cowboy boots, and well-groomed types in three-piece suits.

Inside, under the dim light of a couple of neon bulbs too weak to reach every corner of the structure, eight red plastic chairs, five yellow ones, two black, and an orange one, all in need of first aid, face each other across fourteen tables of various descriptions. John Wayne's likeness guards one wall. Elvis, "The King of Rock'n'Roll," decorates another, while on another John and Robert Kennedy are eulogized on a bright red rug hung higher than everything else.

There are very few items on the menu, which is neatly written in chalk on a two- by three-foot blackboard touting "Coca-Cola-The-Pause-That-Refreshes." This is the first law of good eats: If there are less than six items on the menu, chances are they'll all be delicious. Today's menu reads as follows:

SLICED BEEF $2.85

CHOPPED BEEF $2.75

RIBS $4.50

HOT LINK SANDWICH $2.75

PICKLES .50

SEVEN-UP PIE   SWEET POTATO PIE

The second law of good eats is less frequently observed: If the kitchen is larger than the restaurant, you've most certainly come to the right place. Slick's kitchen not only consists of the usual refrigerator and sink, but extends outdoors to include two huge spits and a two-and-a-half-acre garden. The spits are as large and as black as the hull of the *Titanic*. Slick designed them himself and had them built. Today one is filled with turkeys (for tomorrow's lunch) and the other with sides of ribs. Slick uses tons of hickory wood, which he purchases at $35 a rick. The thunderous hickory fire cooks the rotating meat slowly and evenly and gives it a tangy aroma.

Near the spits, watermelon, cabbage, onions, tomatoes, and canta-loupe grow in neat rows under a hot and merciless sun. Large plastic bags of aluminum cans are stored in the back, a few of them split open, their contents spilling into the cabbage patch. Some of the cans are half-buried in the dirt, giving the impression that someone is try-ing to grow Coca-Cola cans.

Slick neither corroborates nor denies the rumor that he has part ownership of a beef ranch in the vicinity. He is known to be aloof about his finances. Jim Leake says that Slick has been paying the whole year's rent every year for the past twenty-five on January first. "Without fail, Slick shows up in my office with a paper bag full of money." Says Leake, "He pays the rent for the whole year, all $6,000 of it, because I think he's afraid I might raise it otherwise." Another one of Slick's eccentricities is replacing the waitresses every few months. "This is so they won't learn the secret formulas for his two sauces," offers Jim's daughter Jean.

Today, Slick opened at eleven o'clock and already the smell of barbe-cued meat has filled the air around the building and the adjoining dirt parking lot. I take a booth in the corner and order the ribs, the sau-sages, the sliced beef, and a Coke. Vanessa Griffin, a very pretty twenty-five-year-old waitress, brings my order, the customary wax paper, and a ton of paper napkins. She offers two sauces—the hot one is in a yellow mustard container, the mild one in a red plastic ketchup bottle. Both sauces are reddish brown and taste like they have mus-tard, ketchup, pepper, and other spices in them. (Slick is not telling.)

There's enough food on the table for several fools, but I've decided to skip dessert and bread. I've also kind of promised myself to skip dinner (a promise I've broken a thousand times before). The meat on the ribs is rich and tender. It has a strong barbecue flavor and hardly needs the sauces. The sausages have a spicy edge and are the best I've ever had, better than the best ones I've eaten in Germany and England. The sliced steak is flawless—in New York it would cost more than the rent.

Overleaf: Although technically barbecue can be any meat that is cooked by dry heat, in Texas it definitely means beef; this live-stock auction is in Amarillo.

99

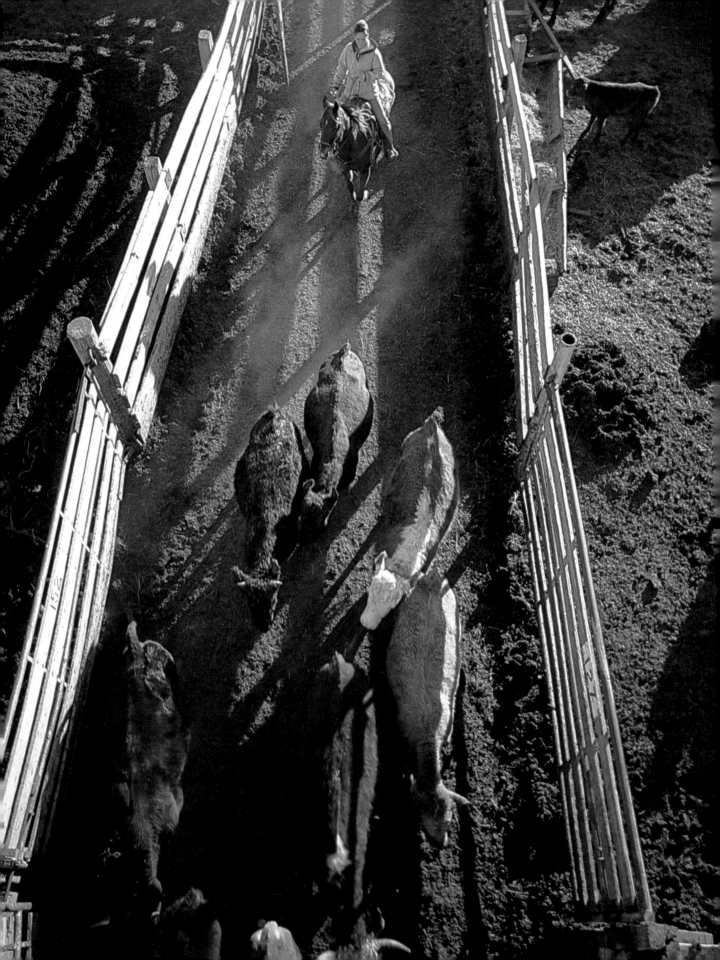

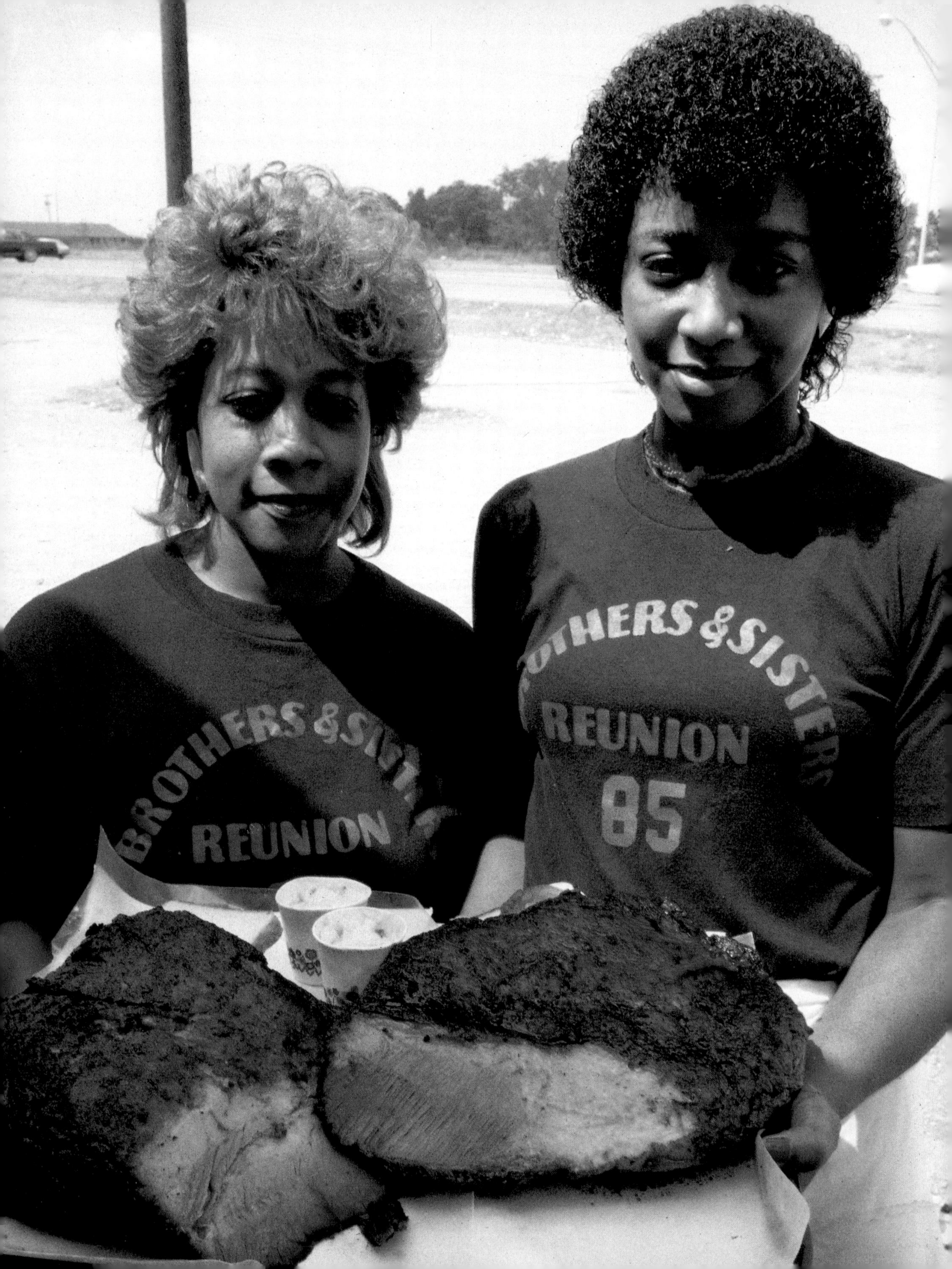
BROTHERS &SIS
REUNION
OTHERS &SISTERS
REUNION
85

Vanessa brings more bread and onions. To my relief, she doesn't seem half as grossed out by my caveman performance as I thought she would be. Within minutes there is a huge mess on the table, bones picked clean, stained napkins, and empty Coke cans. My clothes will need washing in heavy industrial detergent, and I feel like I've betrayed forty years of civilized upbringing and decent training.

Josephine Granger, Slick's sister-in-law and the one who cooks the sweet potato and seven-up pies, comes in as I'm surveying the wreck on my table. She can't remember where and when she learned the recipes for the pies; it feels like she's been making them forever, says Josephine.

Slick's twelve-year-old grandson Adrian letters the menu on the blackboard and adds the prices as Slick dictates them. Adrian also cleans up after the customers—simply by rolling up the wax paper with everything in it. The process seems miraculously efficient: no dishes, no utensils, no tablecloths.

The restaurant will be open until ten o'clock tonight. Vanessa and Adrian will go home, but Slick will be here cooking and serving every single portion himself for the next several hours, as he does six days a week.

Alonzo "Slick" Smith, a stocky black man with sad eyes and large, calloused hands, was born in Muskogee about sixty-five years ago. (According to Vanessa, "He's not going to tell you the truth, I wouldn't even ask him.") He was so good at shooting marbles that one of the neighborhood kids dubbed him "slick" and the name stuck.

He was a farmer and a construction worker before he bought the restaurant. At first, most of the patrons were black farmers and workers. But good food can't be kept a secret in Oklahoma any more than in Paris or Cairo. In no time, people who wouldn't sit together in church or play on the same baseball team were saying "pass the sauce, friend." If there are arguments today, they tend to be about the origins of the word "barbecue" and about what real barbecue is and what it isn't.

Such squabbles have been common, it seems, since men cooked

Opposite: Jackie Ragsdale and Vanessa Griffin display platters of Slick's fabulous barbecued beef. (J. C. Suarès)

Overleaf: Coke is it. A trio of vintage trays represents just about all the interior decoration you'll find at Slick's. (J. C. Suarès)

The Big Texan in Amarillo is a saloon that offers 20-ounce steaks to cowboy and oil executive alike.

their first barbecue in Virginia 400 years ago. According to historical accounts, a dressed and quartered pig was cooked for half a day over hickory coals in a four-foot-deep, brick-lined hole in the ground. The system hasn't changed since, except that the smoke from mesquite, oak, Hawaiian kiawe, and grapevine clippings are also used today, depending on where you are. But who had the idea for the pit in the first place? Was it the West Indies Indians, or was it the Mexican Indians? Or was it the North American plantation slaves?

Here are some clues: "Barbacoa" means "grill" in Spanish; however, the late James Beard said that the word "barbecue" was most likely related to the French expression "*barbe-a-queue*," meaning "from beard to tail." It is also true that meat was cured on plantations by using hickory coals.

In the Southeast, barbecue means pork; in Texas, it means beef brisket or ribs. In the Southwest, they also barbecue chicken, turkey, deer, goat, and mutton. In other words, barbecue is anything that is cooked with smoke instead of steam or fire.

The U.S. Department of Agriculture defines barbecue as "[meat that] shall be cooked by the direct action of dry heat resulting from the

At the Rib Factory in Long Beach, California, a heaping platter of pork ribs necessitates separate dishes for the barbecued beans and potato salad.

burning of hard wood or the hot coals therefrom for a sufficient period to assume the usual characteristics . . . which include the formation of a brown crust. . . . The weight of barbecued meat shall not exceed 70 percent of the weight of the fresh uncooked meat. . . ." That definition has been around since the early 1900s and is based on the way most people cooked barbecue then. Today, that definition and especially its 30 percent shrinkage requirement have caused trouble for companies like Smokaroma, Inc. of Boley, Oklahoma, which makes a machine that pressure cooks 45 pounds of meat in 45 minutes. The meat tastes barbecued, but it hardly shrinks. A few years ago the Department of Agriculture definition was used to enforce truth-in-menu laws in California, and restaurants using Smokaroma equipment were told to stop calling themselves barbecue outlets. Smokaroma has been challenging the decision ever since.

According to food critic John Mariani, who was head judge at the most recent National Rib Cook-Off in Cleveland, Ohio, the best barbecued meat is black on the outside and tender on the inside. Sauces are used to baste the meat while it cooks, and more sauces should be served with the cooked meat. And there isn't a restaurant that doesn't claim a secret sauce formula.

Success doesn't seem to faze Slick. Long black and silver limousines and gold watches and diamond rings don't impress him. He could have had the place redecorated and the broken chairs replaced, but it just doesn't seem important enough. A few years ago, a reporter from the London *Times* stopped by and wrote a rave review of the place. Slick has also been written up in the Tulsa paper and in a couple of magazines. I asked if he saved any clips from those stories. He nodded and disappeared into the kitchen. Adrian showed up a little later bearing a yellowed photostat from a page of the February 1979 *Oklahoma Monthly*. The piece started with a slug, "continued from page 32." I didn't ask for page 32, because it all finally became clear then. Slick can't read or write. He is also the most famous cook in Oklahoma, and he makes better ribs than anyone else in the world.

GUMBO

by John Sturman

There are days when the air in Louisiana's bayou country is so thick and heavy that you can practically cut it with a machete. The forests here are dense and steamy, and tendrils of cypress and Spanish moss trail along the surface of the warm waters, where alligators lazily glide. This is Cajun territory, a distinctive, almost primeval, region where a dialect of French is still widely spoken and unique culinary traditions still prevail.

The word "Cajun" is derived from "Acadian," a term that refers to the French colonists who settled in present-day Nova Scotia and eastern New Brunswick back in the seventeenth century. In 1713 the Acadians were booted out of southeastern Canada by the British, and they set sail for Louisiana, where their descendants still cling to French culture and customs. (The term "Creole" may be used synonymously with "Cajun," although it has several other meanings—for example, it may refer to Louisianians of mixed black and French ancestry or to West Indians of European, usually Spanish, descent—and, though more imprecise, it suggests the fascinating blend of cultures that have helped to shape modern Louisiana.)

One notable feature of Cajun society is that both men and women become skilled cooks. During the hunting season, Cajun men go off to the bayous where, on houseboats that sleep a dozen or more, they drink beer and cook what they catch. René Leonard is a good example. Now in his fifties, he has been cooking since he was a teenager,

Opposite: Much of the fish and crawfish taken from the bayous of Louisiana travels no farther than the tables of local Cajun restaurants.

Overleaf: The Rainbow Inn in Pierre Part, Louisiana, turns out such regional delicacies as fried alligator.

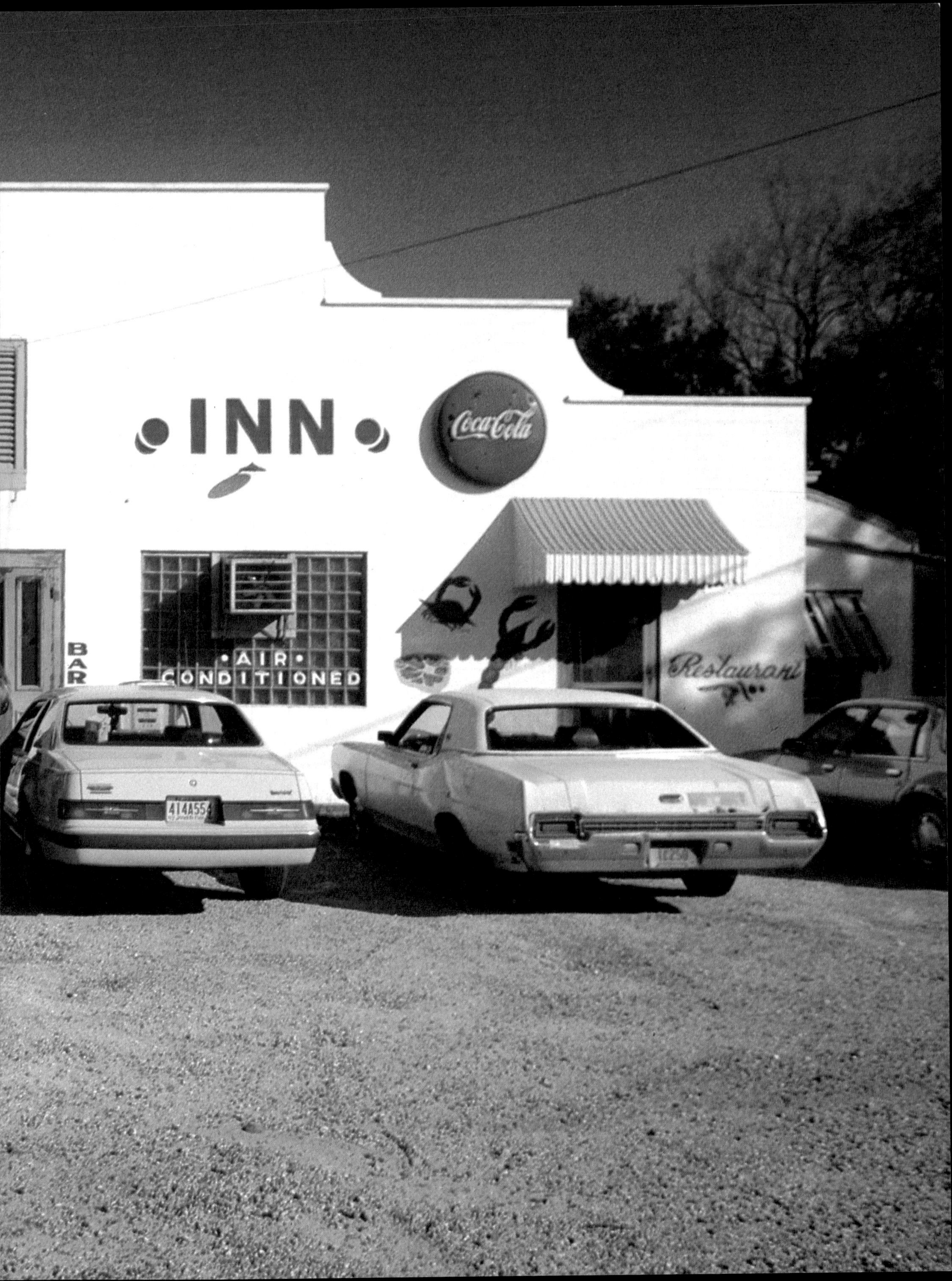
INN
Coca-Cola
AIR
CONDITIONED
BAR
Restaurant

and he has perfected an unusual list of specialties. One is squirrel and spaghetti with sauce piquant; another is deer stew made with a brown roux and Miller Lite beer and served with turtle sauce piquant over spaghetti. René runs the bar at the Rainbow Inn, a whitewashed building some sixty years old on Highway 70, alongside a bayou in Pierre Part, near some of the best hunting and fishing grounds in Louisiana. René's wife, Cora, runs the restaurant, and their daughter Susan Landry now does most of the cooking.

Susan uses skills and recipes she has learned from her parents to produce simple but excellent fare. She turns out such regional treasures as hot sausage with red beans and rice, fried alligator, and fried catfish. Sometimes she cuts the alligator's tail into long strips, coats it with flour and seasoning, and drops it into hot oil in a heavy iron skillet. She also grinds up the tail to make patties, or *boulettes*, as they are called in Cajun French, and bite-size morsels that she calls Alligator McNuggets. Susan's freshwater catfish, also known as tenderloin in these parts, are filleted, fried with yellow flour mixed with corn meal, and seasoned with salt, pepper, and French's mustard. They're cooked in hot oil until they're golden brown and crumble to the touch. They are simply delicious.

But Susan's real specialty is crawfish, and she will only hint at what goes into her bisques and stews. These are family secrets, but to taste these dishes is to discover the true pleasures of shellfish cuisine. Crawfish (often called crayfish) are closely related to lobsters, but they live in fresh water, unlike their larger, marine cousins. In texture, they fall somewhere between lobster and shrimp. Crawfish are usually picked by hand, but when the water level of the Mississippi Spillway is high, they are caught with traps and nets. The crawfish season starts in January, when the shells are soft and easy to pick. By the end of the season, in June, they are tougher and hard on the fingers. "At the start of the season," Susan Landry says, "Mama buys five sacks and has all the children over to pick 'em. We pick four sacks, and she boils the fifth for us to eat. It's a nice way to get us to pick 'em."

No posted menu is needed to announce house specialties at the Rainbow Inn.

A pinch of pepper and a dash of hot sauce spice up Cajun-style chicken.

The Rainbow Inn draws a real working-class crowd. During hunting season, you can watch the deer hunters come in from the bayous for lunch, their pick-up trucks pulling their boats and showing off their booty. But across the Mississippi Spillway, halfway between Baldwin and Jeanerette on Highway 182, is the Yellow Bowl Restaurant, which attracts local and visiting gentry when they feel like dressing down. The clientele includes the McIlhenny brothers, two dapper septuagenarians in white suits whose family developed Tabasco sauce, and art historians who come to the area to study its gracious antebellum plantation homes. The bright-yellow building has stood here since 1927, luring in local businesspeople, sugar-mill managers, and travelers passing through en route between New Orleans and Lafayette. You're likely to hear someone say, "Had my first date at the Yellow Bowl thirty years ago!"

The present owner of the Yellow Bowl is Pat Schrader, a Wisconsin native in his late thirties. Pat is a purist, and everything at the Yellow Bowl is made from scratch. His invaluable right hand is "Mama" Clara Mathews, a grandmother in her seventies who has worked at the Yellow Bowl for some thirty-five years. Pat and Clara maintain a lively banter as they whisk around the kitchen. Small bowls of chopped green and white onions and green bell peppers ("the Holy Trinity— we use them in everything") stand at the ready near the stove. Plastic gallon containers hold two-day roux, in gelatin form after overnight refrigeration, that waits to be mixed into crawfish stew. Fresh, pond-fed crawfish meat, packed in its own fat, is delivered regularly by Bon Creole Seafood Wholesalers. (At the Rainbow Inn, mind you, they look down on crawfish that's not picked in the wild.)

Favorite dishes at the Yellow Bowl include the seafood gumbo, consisting of shrimp and crabmeat cooked in a cocoa-brown roux. (A roux is a sauce made from flour, corn oil, chopped white and green onions and garlic, if desired, chopped red and green bell peppers, and water, red wine, or beer; this heady concoction can simmer for anywhere from 45 minutes to 2 days, depending on the chef and the desired end product.) The crawfish etouffé, a type of stew that takes

Above and below: The Yellow Bowl has been attracting connoisseurs of Cajun cooking since 1927.

Overleaf: Hunting dogs wait patiently for their owner to finish lunch.

only 20 minutes from start to finish for 10 pounds of the small crustaceans, is another highlight of the menu.

There are many other specialties here, including two notable, hearty soups. The gumbo Zab (or "Catholic gumbo") is made with seven kinds of greens—equal quantities of collards, mustard greens, turnip greens, spinach, green onions, fresh parsley, and romaine or green-leaf lettuce—and a stock made from *andouille* (chitterling) sausages, ham, and *taso*, a kind of smoked pork chop. The elaborately seasoned turtle soup features ground turtle meat cooked with carrots, celery stalks, and yellow and green onions in a thick combination of chicken, beef, and seafood stocks. Clara also whips up puff pastries, molded with an ash tray, that she stuffs with wild rice, crawfish meat, red and green peppers, and artichokes.

In the past few years, Cajun cooking has burst from its point of origin and has spread across the United States with the fiery intensity of hot sauce. Today, it is one of the trendiest cuisines around. New York City can quite suddenly boast of at least a dozen Cajun restaurants.

Although I am not normally given to follow the vagaries of food

"Mama" Matthews makes a seafood gumbo with both shrimp and crabmeat at the Yellow Bowl.

fashion—*nouvelle cuisine*, for instance, left me *froid*—I must admit that it's nice not to have to go to Lousiana every time I feel an urge for that state's culinary delights. One of the most successful and distinctive of Manhattan's new spate of Cajun restaurants—and one of my great favorites—is the Gulf Coast, right on the Hudson River at the corner of West and West 12th Streets. This is the fringe of the West Village, an area of disused elevated railroad tracks and abandoned warehouses that are now being converted into expensive condominiums. The neighborhood is still something of an urban wilderness—there are bustling meat-packing plants just a block or two away—but when you're sitting in the Gulf Coast on a warm summer evening, watching angry storm clouds brew over the river, you can close your eyes, inhale the intoxicating aromas of Cajun food and imminent downpour, and easily imagine yourself on a Louisiana bayou in hurricane season.

The best time to go to the Gulf Coast, I've learned from experience, is right when they open. They fill up fast, and I've had to wait an hour or so for a table when I've arrived at 8 or 9 P.M. on a weekend evening. Reservations are not accepted here, and the likes of Calvin Klein and Mick Jagger have had to wait in line, just the same as everyone else.

But although the place has been known to attract media celebrities, it is genuinely friendly and informal—an example of "down-home chic." It is self-consciously done up to look like a roadside diner, with authentic road signs, menus, old photos, Louisiana State pennants, and other memorabilia. The walls are painted in '50s-revival pink and turquoise, there is a handsome wooden bar, and the waiters and waitresses all look like—and probably are—aspiring actors, actresses, and models. On one of my visits, a friend's question about the roux was met by a pleasant but uncomprehending, "The what?"

But no matter. The chef knows what he's doing, and the food here is the real thing. You are seated at a '50s Formica table with plain paper placemats; the silverware comes wrapped in a thin wax-paper bag. You are brought a bowl of cole slaw and some Saltines, and you are offered a drink. Many people go for the blue margaritas, which

Opposite: Ground fish and spices are combined in patties, or *boulettes*, then fried.

you can stir with a blue plastic swizzle stick in the shape of a swordfish. Some appetizers are specials of the day; these have included fried alligator or frogs' legs, which are deep-fried, served with a hearty, peppery milk gravy, and are almost a meal in themselves. Other starters are always available. For instance, there's West Indies salad, which features marinated crabmeat, and a fine gumbo, a soupy, highly seasoned mixture of chopped ham, shrimp, and okra—okra itself, in fact, is also known as "gumbo"—that is also offered in larger quantity as an entrée. I like it so much that I've been tempted to have it for both courses on the same visit.

Along with the gumbo, the main courses that are fixtures on the menu include crawfish etouffé, fried catfish, ribeye steak—a slab of beef of exceptional quality cooked over a mesquite grill (*not* a Cajun tradition)—and chicken and dumplings, which comes with appetizing hot biscuits. The entrées are served with two vegetables, which vary somewhat from day to day. They are likely to include corn pudding—kernels off the cob in an egg-and-milk mixture—black-eyed peas, collard greens, green beans cooked with fatback, and dirty rice. This last offering features white rice mixed with chicken giblets and seasoning.

A frequent—and extremely popular—daily special at the Gulf Coast is blackened redfish. Also known as red drum, redfish are native to the southern Atlantic coast and especially to the Gulf of Mexico. They are abundant in the waters off Louisiana in October and November, but due to skyrocketing demand, shortages have recently been reported. Traditionally, blackened, or peppered, redfish is made in a seasoned cast iron skillet over a burning hot flame; no other type of metal can so effectively withstand the heat required (roughly 700°F). The fish is coated with black pepper and other spices and is tossed into the ungreased skillet until it is cooked, which takes only minutes. At the Gulf Coast, though, they simply throw the peppered fish over their mesquite grill. It looks like a huge charred hunk on your plate, but what it lacks in visual appeal it makes up for in taste. It is as flavorful and succulent as a perfect rare steak.

Gaining admission to Pookie's Creole Kitchen resembles trying to enter a speakeasy during Prohibition. (Both: Ronald Saunders)

Desserts at the Gulf Coast are also worthwhile, if you still have room; the sight of dozens of obviously diet-conscious diners chomping away on chocolate pecan pie or bourbon bread pudding should be an encouragement. One especially good choice that I stumbled on—it's not on the menu but is often a special of the day—is the buttermilk pie, a shallow but surprisingly moist and extremely tasty layer of custard filling topped with whipped cream. As at any self-respecting roadside eatery, you are offered limitless refills of coffee. Or you can follow the Southern example and stick to iced tea.

A 1985 survey of American eating habits revealed that 25 million Americans had recently eaten Cajun food and that another 25 million were interested in doing so. Because of its great popularity, Cajun cooking can now be found along roadsides and in city neighborhoods throughout the country. Unlike the Gulf Coast in almost every respect—except the quality of the food—is Pookie's Creole Kitchen, in the Fruitvale district of Oakland, California, a predominantly black neighborhood of small homes and neat lawns. You could drive by Pookie's a thousand times and never pay it much mind, except perhaps to comment on its rather intimidating exterior. There are no windows, and you must enter through a heavy iron gate that triggers a menacing buzzer when opened. Only the crude, hand-lettered signs announcing that *boudin* (a type of blood sausage) and Louisiana head cheese are available suggests that gastronomic delights await within. Even then, only a small number of aficionados will perk up.

I was first brought here by friends who live in the Bay area and who know what good food is. Even so, when I first walked in, I wondered whether we should just beat a hasty retreat. You stand in a small anteroom and contemplate large signs that are not what you'd call inviting: "We Reserve the Right to Refuse Service to Anyone." "No Bare Tops, No Bare Bottoms, No Bare Feet." Then a small panel in the wall slides open, and, depending on the time of day, you state either that you are interested in having lunch or that you have a reservation for dinner. (Reservations are essential in the evening.) An impassive eye appraises you levelly and silently for a few seconds; then the panel slams shut. You begin to wonder if you've given the wrong password. You consider the possibility that you've walked into a Prohibition-era gangster movie.

Once you are admitted to the restaurant, though, all the cautious reserve melts away, and you are treated almost like a long-lost relation. The place is never very crowded, and Pookie seems to like it that way. The menus for lunch and dinner are identical, and both meals here are leisurely, unhurried affairs. Pookie herself often comes out of the kitchen to check with the diners that everything is all right, sometimes laying a motherly hand on yours. The rest of the staff shares her quiet, soothing, almost tender concern.

The interior of Pookie's is dimly lit. The tables along either wall have red tablecloths; those in the center are covered with red-and-white checked tablecloths. When your main course is brought to your table, the waiter or waitress sets up a small, portable serving table that is brimming over with appetizing dishes. On the basis of a couple of visits and sample bites of what everyone at the table was eating, I can assert that the food is superb. Entrées run the gamut from red beans with rice and spicy sausage to hot Cajun shrimp, jambalaya (a mixture of shrimp, diced ham, and rice cooked in a highly seasoned sauce), and such exotica as stewed turtle. Even relatively simple dishes are memorable; the breaded pork chops, for example, are served with rice smothered in an excellent gravy and buttered squash that is cooked to perfection. Most entrées come with a simple green salad laced with a distinctive, pungent red dressing and hot cornbread and butter. For dessert, you can savor such standards as bread pudding and peach cobbler. When you get up to leave, Pookie and the staff entreat you to come back real soon. I believe they really mean it, and I begin to think about what I'll have on my next visit, even though it'll probably be months before I'm on the West Coast again. When you finally exit after a long, slow, eminently satisfying lunch, you squint in the bright California sun, but you know you've just walked out of Louisiana.

Spicy shrimp stew with mild green peas and sweet peaches.

SPECIALS

by Barbara Ottenhoff

Although we may check into a roadside diner because we are bored and in need of a break or to quell the cry of a sweet tooth, we do most often stop because we are hungry and in need of sustenance. Depending on where we've stopped, whether by force or choice, we find sustenance and comfort in familiar burgers, doughnuts and coffee, sandwiches, milkshakes, or even crackers from the vending machines. But, more than anything, we hope to find a special—blue plate special, special of the day, chicken special, fish special, meatloaf special. A special that will feed our bodies and souls if it doesn't break our hearts.

Not that we don't fill up on burgers or fish and chips or soups and sandwiches when we have to, but, truth be told, when it's seven or eight at night and we've worked hard or traveled far, we hope most of all to pull up a chair at the family table. Maybe the family table without the family and maybe not the table at your family's house, but the family table as painted by Norman Rockwell, the table at Beaver's house or at the Waltons'. We want a dinner cooked by Mom—the Mom who likes to cook and wants to feed us. The Mom who fries chicken and makes biscuits. Mom who cooks broccoli just until it's bright green and mashes potatoes with cream and butter. Mom who disappears into the kitchen to return with a fresh berry pie and slices large wedges just for us. Mom who understands that good food makes the world seem a friendlier place.

Above and below: While the quality of diner specials may be uneven, the quantity is predictable.

The special is home cooking when you can't be home. The first special devised probably came right off someone's family table. It achieved its finished form in the early 1900s and hasn't changed much since—except that, of course, the quality has gone steadily downhill. The menu for the blue plate special in a New York restaurant in 1930 is nearly identical to the menu for the special special at a diner I sometimes stop in on the way home from work. Soup to start, meat, potatoes, vegetable, and beverage. The classic formula has further restraints, however. The soup for a special is mostly vegetables and broth; maybe a meat bone is thrown in the pot in pork or beef country or a piece of fish or a couple of clams on either of the two coasts. The meat is never fancy or expensive. Meatloaf is common across the country, but, in Pennsylvania, it's practically the only special you'll find. Beef liver used to be big, but you don't see it so often anymore. Chicken is common; a pork chop, less so. Occasionally it's a stew made from the tougher cuts of beef.

The vegetable is usually green; sometimes you get two. Peas and carrots are the standard. The potatoes are sometimes mashed, sometimes boiled. Usually there's a lot of gravy over and under everything, unless the gravy is good and then there's just a bit pooled in the center of the mashed potatoes. Portions are always large, but there's usually room for dessert. We hope it's homemade pie. Specials all sound pretty much the same, but it's Mom's cooking that makes the special special, and finding a good special these days is as hard as finding a Mom who still cooks.

I'd love more than anything to have a foolproof system for spotting a place with a good special, for I am passionately devoted to good home cooking, but I don't think there is a system. The only rule for eating on the road that has proven infallible over the years is never eat in a diner attached to a gas station. My theory is that when the gas jockey gets old and arthritic, they move him inside to cook specials.

A name tells nothing. Mom's Diner doesn't guarantee that Mom didn't split years ago to soak up the sun in Florida. Even the adver-

Above and opposite: Roadside diners often have themes, which are carried out in the architecture, decor, and menu. The nautical motif has always been popular.

tisement under the name—"Fresh Fish Daily" or "Charcoal Broiled Steaks"—isn't necessarily true. Apparently there's no truth-in-advertising statute when it comes to signs on diners or restaurants. I go to a diner that advertises "Home-Baked Desserts Are Our Specialty" once in neon under the name, twice on the front door, and at least three more times in the menu. The same home-baked desserts have been in the pastry case for as long as I can remember. Everybody knows better than to order one, or they quickly learn.

Some people tell me a sure-fire sign of getting a decent meal in a place on the road is to check the parking lot for local license plates. The premise is, of course, that if the locals keep coming back the food must be good. This makes sense on the surface, but then there's Jimmy's—a promising-looking place I went to with a friend of mine in Michigan farm country.

Jimmy's customers were indeed locals—I recognized quite a few of them from the hardware store and the feed lot. The food was cheap, as I recall, real cheap, and the steaks did indeed flop over the edges of their platters, which were, truly, THIS big (as my friend had reported). Jimmy and his mom knew almost everyone, and Mom even took so warmly to us newcomers that she showed us the obscene Santa Claus Christmas card before the night was over. A couple of weeks later I read in the local paper that Jimmy's was shut down for selling horse meat. The Saturday night after it reopened, I happened to drive by about dinnertime. The line of locals was just as long as before Jimmy's run-in with the law. So much for the local-license system.

There's another strategy someone tried to explain to me once that starts with, Add the number of Fords to the number of Chevys, then multiply by the number of police cars, and add or subtract the number of trucks, I can't remember which. Probably add—this person's faith in the truck driver's palate being a great deal stronger than mine.

Mary McCrank's Dinner House, which has a terrific reputation among home-cooking devotees in the state of Washington, doesn't do much business with policemen or truck drivers or even locals. Yet Mary McCrank's does a very good business, and has for the last fifty years, serving specials of the sort your mother made or you wish she had.

Nobody just happens to drive by Mary McCrank's. It's four miles off I-5 in Chehalis, and you'd better know where you're going because it's just one house in the middle of Washington farm country. Chehalis is about one hundred miles north of Portland, one hundred miles south of Seattle, and forty miles from Olympia, so that if you live in Olympia, a drive to Mary McCrank's would be just the thing for a Sunday afternoon. Or if you are traveling from Seattle to Portland or vice versa and you time the trip so that you can arrive at Mary's during the lunch or dinner hours, you can consider yourself most fortunate of all travelers.

Mary did most of the cooking for those fifty years, and her old age was indeed a cause for concern. Anyone who ate at Mary's wanted her to go on cooking specials forever, but since she didn't—she died in 1984—the next best thing happened. The house, as well as Mary's recipes and collection of porcelain ducks, teapots, plates, and bric-a-brac, has gone to Raelene and Leonard Guy. The Guys have put a picture of Mary in the menu to assure the customers and have gone on making the iron-skillet fried chicken and sour cream raisin pie just as Mary would if she could be there herself. The specials at Mary's exemplify everything that good specials should be. The ingredients are fresh, and in this farm country they can't get any fresher; the food is simply prepared and cooked with obvious care. Mary's is as close as you can get to pulling up a chair to the family table without actually being there, which is even better sometimes. At Mary's, Mom serves just three beverages—coffee, tea, and buttermilk—and she prefers you not smoke in the house. Unlike Mom's, though, if you stuff yourself at dinner, you can't save the dessert that comes with the meal for later. If you can't eat it there, you have to leave it for someone else.

Mom in the kitchen is what has made Mary McCrank's a success, but Mom at the cash register is what works for Jamie's in Oak Park, Illinois. This small restaurant, just on the right side of the El track in north Oak Park, serves wonderful specials. Situated on the corner of South Boulevard and Oak Park Avenue, Jamie's was Jamie's Sandwich Shop until 1979, when it was bought by Jamie Wilk (a happy coincidence) and her two sons, John Alway and David Degand. In 1984 they expanded into the building next door, so that now Jamie's has a split personality. It is pure diner—with linoleum floor, vinyl-covered booths, Formica tables, and a lunch counter with twelve

Overleaf: Blazing in neon, the Tennessee-Alabama near Kimball, Tennessee, offers everything but the kitchen sink.

Below: The diner we frequent most lies not more than ten miles from home and offers good, cheap specials.

Above and opposite: In between the malls and fast-food chains, diners offer a bit of visual poetry along our highways.

stools—in the original building, and a handsome restaurant with antique oak tables and chairs from Wisconsin in the expansion.

If, when you first walk into Jamie's, you notice that the chef is wearing a toque, you might think there's a wit in the kitchen. But that's Ventura Gonzales, a professional chef trained in French cuisine, whom the mother and two sons hired about three years ago. Gonzales has brought Jamie's from good home cooking to the sublime without taking the prices out of the range of roadside eating. Typical of dinner specials at Jamie's are perfectly roasted leg of lamb with fresh green beans and mushrooms and a baked potato; broiled sea perch with a light dill sauce, au gratin potatoes, zucchini sautéed with fresh tomatoes; and poached salmon with cabbage cooked with green peppers and mushrooms, fresh asparagus, and sautéed potatoes. All specials come with soup or salad and your choice of beverage. It's obviously not everyday home cooking, but neither is it stuffy Continental cuisine. The only truly French dish is the appetizer of escargots served in a squash half—which is delicious, by the way. The breads and rolls are made from scratch at Jamie's, as are the soups and most of the desserts. The formula for good food at Jamie's is keeping the talent in the kitchen and Mom up front to keep an eye on the help, and buying ingredients as fresh as they can be found.

It's unlikely that you will happen upon Jamie's by pulling off the Eisenhower Expressway at Harlem Avenue before speeding into Chicago with the same ease you will find yourself in a Howard Johnson's parking lot just off Interstate 80, but it's well worth the effort of navigating the few blocks from Harlem to South Boulevard to find it. Or, if you want one last terrific meal before leaving Chicago, Jamie's is on the way to the airport.

There are other places like Mary McCrank's and Jamie's out there on the road somewhere, but the special we need the most lies not more than ten miles from home. I live in New Jersey, a state some people call the land of the diner. I'm not sure if New Jersey has more diners than any other state, but there does seem to be a disproportionately

Eva Ladd prepares gallons of banana pudding by hand at the Tennessee-Alabama Restaurant.

large number of them. They all look pretty much the same, the menus are all lengthy and offer nearly the same food, the people seem pretty much alike too. Because I'm in need of good home cooking as much as the next person, I've sort of adopted the diner nearest my home—the Pilgrim in Cedar Grove—and have tried to wring a good special out of it. I've not been sorry.

The Pilgrim's main problem is that it is too big. It can easily seat 250 people and still feel spacious. Diners usually have tacky lighting fixtures, or dying plants, or ugly carpeting, or cheap paneling, or fake rock face glued to the walls. That the Pilgrim has all of the above doesn't really bother me. The regular menu for the Pilgrim is four 14-by-11-inch plastic-laminated pages; it covers bagels, waffles, bacon and eggs, Italian specialties, Greek specialties, appetizers, sandwiches, grilled hamburgers, and so on to dessert. The typed sheet of paper clipped to the back lists that day's specials. Skip the plastic laminate and go for the specials is the first rule of thumb for the Pilgrim and for other diners like it.

The specials at the Pilgrim give evidence of there being someone in the kitchen who thinks it's still 1950 and he or she is serving just fifty people a night instead of three hundred. The job of the home-cooking devotee is to find one of the fifty dinners the cook is still making. The work begins by grilling the waitress about what's fresh and what's not. This is the single most frustrating experience of dining at the Pilgrim, but it does get the adrenalin flowing, which does wonders for the appetite. The waitresses are hired for their speed and deftness (necessary for the extraordinary number of dishes they fit on 2½-by-4-foot tables), not because they can distinguish between fresh and fresh-from-the-can. If pressed, they will tell what they get the most orders for. In the case of the Pilgrim, that is roast chicken with stuffing—a special worthy of devotion. But the system quickly breaks down under the pressure of potatoes—home fried, french fried, mashed, or baked—and a choice of four vegetables. Although one can't go wrong with a baked potato, it's hard to resist the chance to find out if the mashed potatoes are real or if they come out of a box. The Pilgrim's

The Petticoat Junction Cafeteria in Mabank, Texas, is a converted train depot.

are real, if a little gloppy. The home fried, despite the name, are the worst. One of the Pilgrim's vegetables is usually fresh, and, to their credit, it's cooked just until you can slide a fork into it and not beyond that point.

I've never seen anything but iceberg lettuce in a diner, and the Pilgrim is no exception, but they do slice a little red onion into the salad and serve it with a decent house dressing. The chicken special has so far been a sure thing at the Pilgrim; the skin is crisp and the flesh tender and juicy. The stuffing that comes with it is decently seasoned but lacks any real spirit. The special special is usually worth ordering too, unless it's fish and then it's invariably frozen.

Dessert is where my system for getting a good meal out of the Pilgrim broke down. I tried the two-pronged approach—one order of baklava because the Pilgrim seems to be owned and run by Greeks, whom I assumed wouldn't serve a bad Greek pastry, and one order of apple pie, which the waitress assured me a lot of people order. The apple pie was the worst I'd ever come across. The baklava would have compelled any good Greek mother to pull the baker by the ear and give him or her a swift kick out of the kitchen. I've simply never had the heart to try any of the other desserts.

Although I'm willing to make the effort to get a good meal out of the Pilgrim because it's near my home, I always hope to be surprised sometime by finding good home cooking in a place that I didn't suspect had it in it. We expect a good special from Mary McCrank's, for it's come by its reputation by years of hard work. Even at Jamie's, if we stopped in one morning for a cup of coffee on the way to work, we would know enough to return that night for dinner. The Pilgrim delights me because it should be so bad but it isn't. We know there aren't many Mary McCrank's or Jamie's out there, but there might be a few more diners like the Pilgrim than we thought. I hope so.

APPLE PIE

by Roy Finamore

There was once a time when I didn't have to look for dessert. It was simply there. I had a mother who would treat me to pound cake and upside-down cake and a grandmother whose chocolate and chiffon cakes were the stuff of dreams. But then I grew up. These two women decided they had better things to do than spend their waking hours producing dessert for me. "Get a job," they told me.

So I did. I had to commute into New York's Grand Central Station every day, and it was there that I first discovered the dessert table. It was in the Oyster Bar and there were linen and silver and polished wood and it was long and there were desserts from one end to the other. Sitting there alone at odd hours, day after day, tasting, savoring—this was some kind of paradise. Promise and fulfillment. Wouldn't it be nice if I had a Lilith to play with.

Well, I knew this woman. Her name was Amelia and she had sharp eyes and even sharper elbows and she loved dessert more than breath. She was the one who had told me about the bakery in the Bronx where you could get the best cannoli—"They fill while you're there," she had murmured. "They don't get soggy." What better? Amelia. Me. The Oyster Bar. Seats at the counter near the dessert table.

Amelia took the train in from Pelham, and her heels clicked as we hurried across the main waiting room, then down to the Oyster Bar. As soon as we stepped through the door, she caught sight of the des-

If it can't be apple pie, order the next best thing.

sert table and stood as one transfixed. Her knees buckled, just a little. She looked a bit like what Bernadette must have looked like out in the yard that first day at Lourdes. Then there was one small, muted exhalation.

"Oh."

But from then on it was down to business. She wanted to sit facing the table, and she called out "Miss!" before we had finished sitting.

"Oh, miss! Can we see the menu for desserts? Thank you.

"No, no, don't go away; tell me what's best. The key lime? Which one's that?—I don't think I can see it. Oh, he didn't? Well, I'm disappointed. But what about that one. The one at the corner of the table that looks like chocolate but maybe it was made in a bowl? A chocolate nougat layer dome? Thank you."

The waitress walked away and Amelia leaned in toward my ear. "Hooohh."

I told Amelia that she could go up to the table, get the word on each dessert from the chef, and then order. She was gone as the words left my mouth. When she came back she said that she hoped I didn't want anything in particular because she wanted to try the chocolate dome *and* the plum tart so that was what she'd ordered. The plates came and we bickered back and forth over whether the pastry in the plum tart was all or part lard and we agreed that since the chef had an accent that made it Continental so it was probably all lard.

When we had finished and had decided that if the plum was so good we had to try the whole-wheat apple and as long as we were ordering why not some rice pudding (I can still picture her expression as she slipped a spoon of pudding with a smidgen of whipped cream into her little mouth)—I knew. There were other dessert tables in the world, maybe as good as this one, and I would spend my life looking for them.

Often I would wake in the middle of the night, my lone mission pulling me from bed. I wandered the streets in search of pastry and found the all-night diner. No dessert table here, but a dessert "carousel." Sparkling glass cylinders, electrically cooled, their slowly re-

Follow the arrow for sweet delights. (Michelle Siegel)

volving shelves filled to capacity.

I was intrigued. The construction of these cakes and pies was such that they could only be called architectural. The taste reminded me of shredded kraft paper aged in linseed oil, with just a hint of ammonia.

"Why?" I cried. "Who would do such a thing to dessert?"

I ran to the library and leafed through stacks of periodicals catering to the food and chemical research markets. The story, once told, was a scandal. In the beginning was the bouffant pie, the trial run, the product of one or two small factories off the Jersey Turnpike. The pie proved profitable and was followed by a foray into something called the Boston Creme. But then the auto industry began to crumple, the economy to teeter, and Detroit turned its eager eye to this fledgling industry. Engineers were called in. New models were designed. Workers were sent to the assembly lines. Soon it appeared that architectural dessert factories would become Michigan's premier employer.

The test model continues to reign supreme. They call it lemon meringue, and it resembles nothing so much as a spaceship. A sandalwood-tinted mound, six inches high, with a sheen that only repeated polishings with Lemon Pledge can bring. Slicing reveals its true beauty, for the meringue sparkles—think of a brand new styrofoam snowball glistening on a Christmas tree—and the filling—a radioactive yellow—quivers.

I admit it. I have returned repeatedly to the dessert carousel, and I've spent hours staring in delicious horror at the revolving shelves. I am awed by the achievements. The many-fruit tart, with a layout as intricate as that of the gardens of Versailles. Chocolate cakes that look like castles. Apple-crumb somethings that look like broken pediments. Puff pastry swans that look like set pieces for a Wagner opera. These food constructions are often jammed so closely together that the shelves begin to look like crooked, darkened streets with Nesselrode skyscrapers and mocha cream museums looming at every turn.

For a time I despaired. The world would become a giant dessert

Preceding overleaf: An artist at work paints on the finishing touches.

city and there would be nothing to eat. But then I remembered my mother, my grandmother. The brave American individual baking away. I took this to heart, and took my stomach on the road once more.

One day I found Louisa's, a tiny café in Cape May, New Jersey, and I spotted the dessert table almost as soon as I walked in. The table was tiny; there were only a couple of desserts huddled together, and one of them was a fruit tart. The menu was tiny, too—just one or two things for lunch, mussels, I think, and they did smell good. But I kept looking back at the tart. It was a pear walnut tart, and it was warm and it was golden with the glow of an apricot glaze. Who needed lunch? I ate the tart, and I was content.

Let's pause a moment and think about eating dessert. Think of the little growls of contentment. Think of teeth and lips stained purple by a tangy blueberry pie. Think of playing in the puddle you can make by putting vanilla ice cream on warm apple pie. Now think of a giant dessert table—big enough to put a roof over.

I found one, hidden away in Ronks, Pennsylvania. There—in the land of the Dutchman's Diner, the Family Style Restaurant, and the Black Angus Beer Fest—is Fisher's Pastries. The giant dessert table.

I had heard rumors of this place, and a friend and I happened to be in the neighborhood. All right, I confess: we set out to find it. After a few hours of driving, Carl and I came across a little wood house with a quaint horse-drawn buggy in front and a hand-lettered sign on the road that read:

> QUILTS FOR SALE
> NOT RESPONSIBLE
> FOR ACCIDENTS
> NO SUNDAY BUSINESS

A half-hour later we tracked down our dessert table. A stand run by the Fisher family, with the youngest Fisher presiding. There was some other stuff that wasn't dessert—rows of gleaming pickle jars, mountains of rich yellow egg noodles, stacks of floury fresh-baked bread. Well, fine, I thought, this must be for the tourists. Me, I made a beeline for the desserts, and Carl was right behind me.

There were sugar cookies and molasses cookies and doughnuts and cheesecake and pie. Oh, was there pie. Raisin pie and rhubarb pie and shoofly pie and coconut molasses and peach and snitz. We asked young Fisher, "What's snitz pie?"

He smiled.

"What's inside?"

He looked over at the corner of the stand, then back at us. Another smile. "Dried apple."

I made a quick decision. "Would you put that over to the side, please? We'll want that."

Carl, ever alert, noticed that they had root beer for sale. Home-

It's comforting to know a second slice is available. (Michelle Siegel)

The sleepy character of Lancaster, Pennsylvania, evokes a simpler time when everything was home-baked. (Michelle Siegel)

made root beer, and not just by the bottle—it was by the glass, too.

In a matter of moments we each had a glass in hand, and we were contemplating the tray of whoopie pies. You may ask (I did): what's a whoopie pie? Two small round chocolate cakes sandwiching white frosting. The grandfather of the Ring Ding. Waiting was now more than either of us could bear. We got refills on the root beer, two whoopie pies each, excused ourselves to young Fisher, and retired to opposite sides of the stand to eat our chocolate in private.

Chocolate cake should be rich, dark, moist, and light; touched by an unskilled hand, it can become heavy and sodden or just sadly dry. The perfect cake needs no icing, no frosting; the coal-black upper crust itself provides more than enough excitement for eager tastebuds. But then, as somebody said (and I wish I could remember who), a little too much is just enough for me.

Mrs. Fisher's whoopie pie cake needs no frosting, but she uses it as almost an option—it's in the middle so you still get to taste the crust. And the cake—just rich enough and moist enough to stick to the roof of your mouth, right behind your teeth.

We are roused from our bliss by a pair of interlopers who had discovered the table and were trying to convince young Fisher to part with *our* snitz pie. The bloodshed was minimal, and the interlopers got off with a blackened eye and the coconut molasses. Dizzy with success, we picked up our snitz, and a peach too, and we were off. We had been driving for about an hour, picking at the crust, when we realized that we hadn't bought out the supply of whoopie pies, we hadn't bought any root beer to take with us, and we had only one pie apiece. But it was getting late, and we knew that by the time we got back to Fisher's the table would be bare.

I cut into the snitz when I got home. The dried apples had been cooked until they were like a heavenly thick apple butter, and the crust was buttery rich top and bottom.

The next day I found someplace new for dessert. No, they don't have a dessert table, but I can sit under a picture of the Coliseum and eat gelato and be content. Almost.

ICE CREAM

by Matthew Klein

The best ice cream I ever had was in 1964 in a small Missouri town whose name I have lost.

In March of that year I hitchhiked from New York to California. I had primed myself for the journey by reading several novels by Jack Kerouac. In one of his books (I think it was *Darma Bums*) Jack spoke of making a trip across the country eating only apple pie and ice cream each time he stopped. He felt that it was a good barometer of the quality of life. I thought it was a good idea but not pure enough. I would eat only ice cream on my trip. The fact that it was early March and very cold didn't occur to me as I made my plans.

I had made it to Missouri without major incident and was trying to hitchhike out of St. Louis on Route 66, at the town line. There was a storm—freezing rain—and no one was stopping for me. Now it is obvious, but then I was oblivious. I never connected my shoulder-length hair and generally disheveled appearance with my lack of success at getting a lift. Anyway, I stood on the corner for two and a half hours when at last a faded green, battered 1952 Plymouth stopped. When I opened the door the driver said, "I'm only goin' 'bout a hunnerd miles down the road, but . . ." Not nearly far enough for me. The next big town was Springfield, about 250 miles away. Anything short of that and I'd have to repeat this experience with less traffic and less chance of getting a ride; but I looked down at my thumb where an icicle was beginning to form. "Great," I said, "thanks a lot." The driver had the heat on full blast, but I sat huddled in my coat with my teeth chattering.

About two hours later we turned off the highway into a small town. I won't go into the jokes about how small it was, but it was *small*. There was only one paved road. It ran perpendicular to the highway for about a third of a mile, then became a dirt, or mud, road. There was a general store and post office, which was also the bus stop. There were a farm supply store (feed, fence posts, small tractors), a barber shop, a couple of other small stores, and a diner. This was a *real* diner—a railroad car on cinderblocks.

The driver left me off at the general store and I went in and asked about the next bus south. By then I had realized that getting a ride from here was going to be tough; I had seen only a dozen or so cars in the last fifty miles. I decided to take a bus to Springfield. It was about one o'clock and the next bus wasn't until three thirty. I figured I could kill a couple of hours in the diner and walked up the road a couple of hundred feet to it. I climbed up the four or five steps. It was wonderful inside! All the surfaces were of wood, painted with about ten thick coats of enamel—white, pale green, and red. There wasn't a bit of stainless steel or Formica in the place. There was a counter and a row of booths recently covered in red vinyl. The few patrons were all men in their thirties or forties. Most were wearing overalls, flannel shirts, and denim jackets.

As I walked in everyone turned and stared at me. I felt their reception was slightly hostile. (I look back on it now and realize that it was very hostile.) I sat down at the booth closest to the door and the waitress came over to take my order. A round white button with big red letters was pinned to her apron: "JO ANN."

"What can I get you, honey?" Well, that wasn't so hostile. I relaxed a little.

"Do you have any ice cream?"

She answered as though it was the most natural thing in the world. "Yes," she said, "the cook just made some yesterday."

"Great! I'd like some, please."

The right stuff. Homemade vanilla ice cream has a purity and a purpose all its own. (Michelle Siegel)

She turned and went behind the counter. I looked out the window. The other customers looked at me. A moment later she was back with a dish of vanilla ice cream unlike any I had seen. It was not white like vanilla ice cream was supposed to be. It was a rich deep yellow and fragrant with vanilla. There were no little black vanilla seeds in it so I don't believe that a real vanilla bean was used, but a lot of vanilla extract must have gone into it. It was just a single round scoop in a small, shallow bowl; no fudge topping, no whipped cream or cherry; no exotic flavor; no ornamentation of any kind. But it was unbelievably good. I could taste separately but simultaneously all the subtle flavors. If the cook had made a gallon of the ice cream, he must have used at least four dozen egg yolks and half a gallon of cream. It was very rich tasting, but not too sweet. I was transfixed, totally unaware of the other customers staring at me. I was having a semi-religious experience.

For the true aficionado, ice cream is a lifetime addiction. (Michelle Siegel)

Overleaf: The perfect hot fudge sundae—before and after. (Matthew Klein)

In the midst of this reverie a shadow crossed my plate . . . and stayed there. I looked up. There was a cop—not your typical big-city-seen-it-all-before cop, but a country ain't-seen-nothin'-like-it-and-don't-want-to cop. He was a little over six feet tall and beefy; not quite fat, but not exactly trim or athletic. He had fair skin, light brown hair, and freckles. He was wearing a hat—something like that of a cavalry soldier—and mirrored sunglasses. There was an ice storm outside. It was dark enough for the three streetlights in the town to be on, and he was wearing sunglasses.

His questions ran together like one, and there was no preamble. "What's your name, how did you get here, where are you going?" I turned pale. This could be Big Trouble. Best to just answer the questions simply. I told him my name, that I had hitchhiked from New York and was on my way to San Francisco via Los Angeles.

The sublime pleasure of a simple ice cream cone.

"Do you have a job in New York?"

"No."

"Do you have a job in San Francisco?"

"No."

"How much money are you carrying?"

"About thirty-five dollars."

"Well, I'm afraid I have no choice but to arrest you for vagrancy. Pay your check and get in the car." He nodded toward a recent model Ford patrol car. I had heard that the penalty for vagrancy in most states was sixty days.

"Can I finish my ice cream?" I asked. By now I was sweating profusely.

"No."

Back in high school I had been a real smart-ass, and the tendency to make sarcastic remarks and wisecracks remained—as did a wide streak of insolence.

"Why not?"

"Because you are under arrest and you can't eat ice cream in police custody."

It was funny. I tried to hide my smile but couldn't. He also must have realized how ridiculous he sounded. He didn't actually smile, but he appeared to soften a bit and said, "OK, but don't take your time." I pushed my luck.

"Would you like some?" And without waiting for a response, I said to the waitress, who, along with all the customers by now, appeared fascinated with my plight, "Would you please bring another for my friend?"

He looked startled, then relaxed and sat down in the booth opposite me. The waitress brought the ice cream over, and only then did the sunglasses and hat come off. Oh, great, I thought, now what do I do? Perhaps open the conversation with, "Hey, I had some great acid last week." No good. "I saw Allen Ginsberg in the Figaro just before I left New York." No good. "I saw this great sculpture that John Chamberlain made out of three wrecked cars." No good.

A race against time at the Country View Drive-In in Sedgewick, Maine.

I bought some time. "Great ice cream, huh?"

"Yeah, the cook makes it himself. He's a real ice cream nut."

"You sure can't buy this in the supermarket."

"No, you can't."

Great conversation! Where do we go from here, I wondered. I remembered what a friend of mine, a real coffee-house intellectual, told me about why he had always followed baseball. "No matter where you go," he said, "or with whom you are trying to relate, everyone knows about baseball."

"I hear the Cards are going to have a great year," I ventured. Magic! His face lit up.

"I tell ya the Cards are going to have a fan*tas*tic year!" We talked about the Cardinals, the Yankees, Mickey Mantle, Ted Williams, and the state of the game in general. I tried to keep to areas that I was familiar with, but soon I found myself mouthing words that had no meaning to me, hoping he wouldn't discover my fundamental lack of knowledge about baseball. We ate our ice cream and ordered more. We talked about baseball for about an hour; then it was time to go. The hat and sunglasses went back on, I paid the check (a dollar and a half), and we left.

Outside he opened the rear door of the patrol car and I got in. It was as I expected: no door handles and a heavy wire screen between the front and rear seats. Well, at least there were no handcuffs or leg irons. We drove in silence out to the highway and stopped. He got out and opened my door. "I'm going to let you go," he said. "I hope I'm not making a mistake. You can wait for the bus here. Just flag him down and he'll stop."

He got back into the car and drove off, spraying the wet gravel with his wheels.

Up the road I could see a pick-up truck coming. I stuck out my thumb and he stopped. "I'm only goin' as far as Tulsa . . ." "Great!" I said, "Thanks."

✦✦✦✦✦✦✦✦✦✦✦✦✦ **CREDITS** ✦✦✦✦✦✦✦✦✦✦✦✦✦

Jill MacNeice started her career as a writer doing the doughnut run at United Press International's Washington, D.C. bureau. Since then she has written *The Group House Handbook*, *101 Ways to Cut Legal Bills*, and *Guide to Historic Sites*, and numerous articles for magazines and newspapers.

Schuyler Ingle writes about food and crime for *The Weekly* in Seattle, Washington. He has written for *Connoisseur*, *Vogue*, *New West*, and *Harper's* and is a contributing editor at *New Age Journal*. Ingle is currently at work on a cookbook for Simon and Schuster.

Ralph Gardner, Jr., is at work on a novel documenting his various vices besides cheeseburgers. His articles have appeared in *Cosmopolitan*, *Penthouse*, *Barrons*, and *The Soho News*. He is also the author of *Young, Gifted and Rich* and the forthcoming *A View from the Top*.

Between meals, **Russell Martin** has written *Cowboy: The Enduring Myth of the Wild West* and co-authored *Entering Space* with

astronaut Joe Allen. *Matters Gray and White*, a profile of a brain specialist, will be published in 1986. He lives in southwestern Colorado, near the "Pinto Bean Capital of the World," and within a three- or four-hour drive of a few good places to eat.

LeRoy Woodson is a photographer and journalist whose work has appeared in *Life*, *Vanity Fair*, *National Geographic*, *Time*, *Newsweek*, and the *Washington Post*.

Ever alert to new developments in the curbside sausage trade, **Timothy White** is a resident of New York's Greenwich Village and author of the bestselling *Catch a Fire—The Life of Bob Marley* as well as *Rock Stars* and a forthcoming history of Southern California. His is happiest when both his writing and his wieners are "on a roll."

J.C. Suarès is a writer, illustrator, and designer whose articles have appeared in *Connoisseur*, *New England Monthly*, *Art and Antiques*, *Harper's*, and *Interview*. Among the subjects he has written about are caviar, chocolate, and lobsters.

John Sturman is a New York-based writer, editor, and art critic. His work can be found in *ARTnews* and other publications; he can be found at an old-fashioned Polish lunch counter in the East Village.

Barbara Ottenhoff cooks her specials—with herbs and vegetables from the backyard garden—in New Jersey and is currently a senior editor at *Good Food* magazine. Previous stops on the road have included editing for *Cuisine* magazine (in Chicago and New York), Harper & Row, Workman Publishing, and Simon & Schuster.

Roy Finamore is a New York-based editor and writer.

Matthew Klein is a food photographer based in New York whose work has appeared in *Time*, *Fortune*, *Saturday Review*, *Discover*, *Psychology Today*, and in many cookbooks. He estimates that he ate twice his weight in ice cream while writing and shooting his book *The Joy of Ice Cream*, which was published in 1985.

RESTAURANTS

The Cadillac Bar
Houston, Texas
(713) 862-2020

Fisher's Pastries
Ronks, Pennsylvania

Garcia's
Albuquerque, New Mexico
(505) 247-9149

Genero's
Gallup, New Mexico
(505) 863-6761

The Gulf Coast
New York, New York
(212) 206-8790

**Hancock's Ogunquit
Lobster Pound**
Ogunquit, Maine
(207) 646-2516

Hattie's Hat
Seattle, Washington
(206) 784-0175

Jamie's
Oak Park, Illinois
(312) 386-3456

Louisa's
Cape May, New Jersey
(609) 884-5882

**Mary McCrank's
Dinner House**
Chehalis, Washington
(206) 748-3662

Mi Tierra
San Antonio, Texas
(512) 255-1262

Nunan's Lobster Hut
Cape Porpoise, Maine
(207) 967-4362

The Old Pancake House
Eugene, Oregon
(503) 344-7830

The Oyster Bar
New York, New York
(212) 490-6650

Papaya King
New York, New York
(212) 369-0648

The Pilgrim
Cedar Grove, New Jersey
(201) 239-2900

The Rainbow Inn
Pierre Part, Louisiana
(504) 252-9043

The Shed
Santa Fe, New Mexico
(505) 982-9030

Slick's
Muskogee, Oklahoma
(918) 687-9215

Teddy's
Paterson, New Jersey
(201) 742-3435

**Thomas House Restaurant
and Air-Conditioned
Home Bakery**
Dayton, Virginia
(703) 879-2181

Vallejo's
Colorado Springs, Colorado
(303) 635-0980

The White Manna
Hackensack, New Jersey
(201) 342-0914

Composed in Bodoni Book by
TGA Communications Inc.,
New York, New York.
Printed and bound by
Novograph, s.a., Madrid.